"Mariel Davenport together a Bible study that is an enjoyable journey to knowing God more deeply simply through studying the many facets of His names. The study is wonderfully prepared, with Greek and Hebrew placed in a context we can understand and a daily regimen we can actually complete, even with a busy schedule."

Beth Patch, Spiritual Life Devotions
Editor, CBN.com

"Mariel Davenport is one of those rare and anointed authors who can cause Scripture to come alive. As she unpacks the Word of God, she applies the truths contained therein in a way that speaks directly into the heart of the reader. My heart is always blessed when I read her work. Always!"

Leah Adams, author, speaker,
founder of The Point Ministries

"The study of Knowing God Through His Names helped me understand the thread woven from the Old Testament into the New Testament with God's names. From the very primitive names the early Israelites invoked begging for mercy to the precious name of Jesus the people called out asking for yet another miracle. Thanks to the author's simple language and the depth of this study I have come to a deeper relationship with our Lord."

Maria Solano, Bible study participant

"I've sat under Mariel Davenport's teaching and been amazed at how she opens my eyes to truths I have never seen before in passages I've read many times. She has a God-given ability to dig deep into His Word and pull very practical things out that I can apply to my life. I believe Mariel is the next Beth Moore."

Rebekah Furches, Bible study participant

"Emerging from her personal belief of atheism by finding the Great I AM as her personal savior, Mariel teaches Knowing God Through His Names with conviction and clarity. God's name, character, and attributes shine through the pages to reveal His lavish love for each of us. Women of all ages will find this study challenging and encouraging."

Shirley Sharpe, Bible Teacher and attendant study

"This was my first experience to be in a Bible Study that was taught by the author! It was a journey for me. To see Jesus in not only the NT, but also in the OT was a real eye opener for myself. Mariel brings out the importance of understanding that the translation of the Hebrew makes a difference, and actually was teaching us some Hebrew. I highly recommend this study, and I look forward to doing it again."

Linda Cullen, Bible Study participant

KNOWING GOD
THROUGH HIS NAMES

KNOWING GOD
THROUGH HIS NAMES

A Ten Week Study

With Our Unchanging God

MARIEL DAVENPORT

TATE PUBLISHING *& Enterprises*

Published by Tate Publishing & Enterprises, LLC
127 E. Trade Center Terrace | Mustang, Oklahoma 73064 USA
1.888.361.9473 | www.tatepublishing.com

Tate Publishing is committed to excellence in the publishing industry. The company reflects the philosophy established by the founders, based on Psalm 68:11,
"The Lord gave the word and great was the company of those who published it."

Book design copyright © 2010 by Tate Publishing, LLC. All rights reserved.
Cover design by Kellie Southerland
Interior design by Stefanie Rane

Published in the United States of America

ISBN: 978-1-61739-376-1
1. Religion Devotional
2. Religion, General
11.04.15

DEDICATION

To my "Knowing God Ladies" who were the first to stroll through these pages with me.

Thank you all for your love, encouragement, and support. You make me press into Jesus—to increasingly know Him and grow in Him, and for that I am eternally grateful. It is my honor to serve you all. I love you.

ACKNOWLEDGMENTS

I want to acknowledge and thank those who helped me through this project with prayers, love, and support. I could not have gotten to this point without you. Thank you to Tate Publishing for giving me a chance to live my dream.

It was amazing to open this project with my grandmother and mother, Gloria and Maria, by my side. Aba and Mom, thank you for your encouragement and support. What a legacy the Lord is building for our family line! "[The Lord's] people will rebuild the ancient ruins" (Isaiah 58:12).

To my precious sons, Bryan and Matthew, thank you for your flexibility as Mommy follows Jesus. "Follow my example, as I follow the example of Christ" (1 Corinthians 11:1). You are gifts beyond measure, and I love seeing you love Jesus. I love you both!

Thank you to my husband and best friend, Mike, for being willing to get wet in the storms as the Lord sifted me through this project. Thank you for being my biggest fan! I love you.

And finally the richest thank you to my El Shaddai, without whom I would have nothing to pour forth. May You be glorified above all else. I could not love You more, yet I do every day. Thank You for entrusting me with this adventure!

TABLE OF CONTENTS

KNOWING HIS NAME

Why is it significant to study God's names? Names were thought to reveal the essential character and nature of a person—to know God's name is to enjoy a kind of privileged access to Him. By revealing His names, God made Himself not only accessible but vulnerable. Not only could His people call on His name in prayer, they could dishonor it by living in ways that contradicted His character.

Studying and knowing the names by which God reveals Himself in Scripture gives us further insight into the heart of our very accessible God. By His names, His character is revealed.

Consider this: why do we not name our children Jezebel, Adolf, or the name of a bully in school? It is because of name association and name meanings. We don't want our children associated with those names. They conjure up negative images.

Do you know what *your* name means? Or *why* you are named what you are? Most parents search baby name books and the Internet for name ideas for their new bundle of joy. Yet ancient names carried even more significance.

God's names answer to our insecurities, fears, anxieties, and troubles—whatever is going on in our lives, knowing and trusting God's name will meet us right where we are.

So why does He have so many names? In this study, we will only dig into nine of His names, but there are many more. God's character is infinitely more than we can get our hearts and minds around, so He reveals Himself in bite-size nuggets for us to soak in.

We serve a *knowable* God. He expresses this desire to be known in Isaiah 43:10.

> You are my witnesses, declares the LORD, and my servant whom I have chosen, so that you may know and believe me and understand that I am he. Before me no god was formed, nor will there be one after me.

He also sent His one and only Son, Jesus, so we might know Him. He chooses to reveal His names so we can know His heart and character even more intimately. There is trust and security built when we really *know* someone. Such is true when we really get to know our God. Take a look at Proverbs 18:10 and Isaiah 50:10.

In order to grow in our personal relationship with Him through His Son, we need to know Him as He desires to be known. Based on Matthew 7:24–25, our growth can only happen on a steady foundation built on truth. I have heard it said, "What we believe determines how we live." Let's believe truth, and live it out!

Never forget that our response to His names will be crucial. This is not meant to add to our head knowledge but to ignite our hearts to respond.

The fallen world we live in bombards us with lies about God. As believers, we must identify and replace them with truth. Much of what we believe to be true about God is derived from our past experiences, our upbringing, our hurts, and even our victories. In reading Psalm 51:6, we see God desires truth all the way into our inward parts—heart, soul, and mind.

Satan has been deceiving believers from the beginning. Compare the first lie in Genesis 3:1–6 with what God had previously said in Genesis 2:15–17. Do you see how Satan made slight alterations to what God had said? The serpent is doing the same thing with us now. We have to know God well enough to be able to identify those lies.

Nancy Leigh DeMoss makes this point in her book *Lies Women Believe:*

> Satan deceived Eve by causing her to make her decision based on what she could see and on what her emotions and her reason told her to be right, even when it was contrary to what God had already told the couple.[1]

What about us? What are we basing our decisions on? Are we believing God really is who He says He is? Or are we convinced God is not enough? We buy more, eat more, get more, and watch more because we believe God is not big enough. We manipulate, control, and fix every aspect of our husband's life, our children's lives, and our relationships. We keep thinking God doesn't care and we base our decisions on that lie.

His name is above all names, as Philippians 2:9 tells us—meaning His character is above all character and it is wrapped up in Jesus. We will study parallels between the Old Testament and the New Testament in our homework each week. First Kings 9:1–3 teaches us that where His name is, He is. We want to know His names in order to best recognize His presence. But let's keep in mind the truth of Exodus 20:7. God's name is to be held in high esteem. It is holy. Studying His names does not give us permission to take Him lightly. Let's allow this study to bring us to a place of awe and reverence like never before.

Studies have shown that we retain ninety percent of what we can make and manage ourselves. So if we take the time to work out on paper what the Lord is teaching us, we are more likely to retain it and apply it to our lives. I strongly encourage you to practice this habit. When you come to the section labeled "Just Between God and Me", stop and take time to prayerfully journal your thoughts to the Lord each week. Then look forward to how the Lord will use that to change and grow you in your walk with Him. May you find Him to be the thrill of your life as you seek Him on this journey through His names.

MEMORY VERSE:

> Those who know your name will trust in you, for you, Lord, have never forsaken those who seek you.
> Psalm 9:10 (NIV)

Begin in prayer. Ask the Lord to prepare your heart and to open your eyes to see wonderful things in His Word. Then take a moment to write out the memory verse on an index card to carry with you. Practice it this week. In spare moments throughout the day, practice saying the verse to yourself, pray it back to the Lord, and meditate on it frequently.

In the introduction, we learned that much of what we believe to be true about God is derived from our past experiences, our upbringing, our hurts, and even our victories. It is crucial to get to the root of our beliefs about God in order to press it up against the truth of God's Word.

Take a moment to ask the Lord to search your heart. Ask him to reveal what it is you believe about him. Who is He to you? Describe His heart, His activity, and His ways as you see them.

he is our savior our life our everything he talks back too us in every way he is our life and treater

What experiences in your life are coming to mind as you meditate on who you believe God to be—your parental relationships, previous heart aches, losses, seasons of defeat, or pain. Remember that good experiences add to our belief system too!

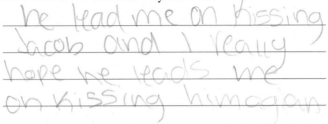

he lead me on kissing Jacob and I really hope he leads me on kissing him again

I pray you have been honest with the Lord. Our false beliefs about Him are not news to Him. He knows the deepest places of our soul. But as we come unveiled before him, he will heal our hurts, apply truth to our lies, and grow us to be more like Jesus in the process.

Read 2 Corinthians 3:15–18. This passage is referring to the unbelieving Jews who have a veil over their eyes, spiritually speaking. Like those Jews, we too can turn to the Lord.

The original Greek word translated "turns" in verse 16 means to turn toward something to embrace it. We are in the same way to turn toward the Lord to embrace Him!

What does the passage say will happen when we do turn to Him in this way?

And what will we reflect when we do?

As we seek to reflect His glory let's get to know Him as He has revealed Himself in Scripture.

Do you know what your name means? Does it define who you are? Names in antiquity defined the nature, character, and even the future of the one named. Our names do not generally carry the significance that names once did. Let's look at an example.

Read Ruth 1:1–22.

The name Naomi means "pleasant and joy." What had happened in her life that caused her to want to change her name from "pleasant and joy"?

_____

_____

What did she want to change her name to?

_____

Her new name meant "bitterness." What reason did *she* give for wanting to change her name?

_____

What could a root of bitterness grow from? Life is hard and filled with disappointments, pain, loss, and plenty of opportunity for us to allow a root of bitterness to grow within our hearts. Scripture warns against this.

Meditate on Hebrews 12:15. It warns us to be aware of bitterness and not allow it to take root within our hearts. Why? (Fill in the verse below according to the NIV.)

See to it that no one misses the _____

_____ ...

When we are unaware of God's true nature and character, we miss His grace toward us. This can lead to the bitterness within us taking root and then growing to defile many—our marriages, our children, our churches, our friends. But when we know Him intimately and we seek to grow in that relationship, we will train ourselves toward godliness which has a promise for us, both in this life and in the one to come. (1 Timothy 4:8.)

Each day after digging into the Word spend a quiet moment before the Lord. As we begin to learn His names, I encourage you to use that name in prayer.

DAY 2

Begin by asking the Lord to speak to you through His Word today, and take a moment to review the memory verse for the week.

Most people in our culture are given a first name, middle name, and a last name; three names for one person. Our first name is generally the name we are called most often. Our last name is our family name and generally given from our fathers. It tells who we belong to. Our middle name, is most often a name given so angry mothers have more words to say when calling their children and warning them they are in trouble.

In his book *Names of God,* Nathan Stone says,

> The great and infinite and eternal God has given us different names to express different aspects of His being and the different relationships He sustains to His creatures.[2]

God, in His infiniteness, has many names, even one we will not know until we are with Him in glory! (See Revelation 19:12.)

Let's begin to look at the power and significance His names carry and how that might make a difference in our life.

Read Psalm 9.

As with many psalms, this is a psalm written by King David. List a few things from this psalm that David knew to be true about God.

_____

_____

_____

_____

_____

_____

According to verse 10, what do those who know God's name do?

_____

What is God's promise according to this verse?

_____

The word "know" in this verse is the Hebrew word *yada*. It means to perceive, understand, know, be familiar with; to know sexually as a husband knows his wife.[3] This is a very intimate knowledge of another. Psalm 9:10 tells us that when we know God's character, nature, and personality as intimately as a husband knows his wife, then we will trust in Him. We will know we are safe with Him.

Meditate on this thought while keeping your heart honest before the Lord. Are you willing to let Him reveal Himself in such a way that this intimacy could be formed between you?

DAY 3

Begin by asking the Lord to speak to you through His Word today, and take a moment to review the memory verse for the week.

Throughout Scripture, God has given us countless "real people" examples of just about anything we could come up against—good, bad, and ugly. When I study Scripture, I like peering into the lives of these men and women. It often sheds light on my own heart, giving me direction and clarity.

There are portraits in Scripture of men and women who trusted in the name of God, and there are those who failed to trust in His name. Often a contrast can be enlightening as we look at our own hearts.

Begin by reading 2 Kings 18:5–8.

What did King Hezekiah trust in?

_____

What three specifics does verse 6 teach us about what it means to trust in the Lord?

- He _____ to the Lord.

- He _____ to follow Him.

- He _____ the Lord had given.

Is this how we are living our lives day in and day out—in the midst of laundry, children, car pool, marriage, work, and dirty dishes?

I so desire my life to be marked by trusting in the Lord! But just as I would not trust someone I just met, I can't trust a God I don't *really* know intimately and through experience.

As a result of his trusting in the Lord, how is Hezekiah described?

_____

Not only was he successful in all he did, but the Lord was with him. What an epitaph this man would have!

Now, let's look at a contrast. Read over the first few headlines of Deuteronomy 1 to get the context, and then carefully read Deuteronomy 1:29–36.

What had the Lord done for the Israelites?

_____

_____

Now fill in verse 32, according to the NIV translation,

In spite of this, you did not _____
in the _____ _____
_____.

How could the Israelites see all the miracles they had seen God perform right before their eyes, and yet not trust Him? Though we may never see some of the miracles the Israelites witnessed, we have certainly seen God's hand at work in our lives in various ways.

I am sure we each have a testimony of how God has worked in our individual lives, whether it was through a new job, financial provision, or a changed heart.

What about you? Jot down a specific example, big or small, where you thought, *that had to be God.*

_____

_____

_____

When we think we are seeing a coincidence, we are actually witnessing the hand of a sovereign God at work in our lives. Yet, despite this, we fail to trust Him when our husband gets laid off, we get devastating news from the doctor, or something happens to rock our world.

We might unfortunately say, "In spite of this, we did not trust in the Lord our God." Why would that be? What keeps us from trusting Him fully? Spend time pondering this before the Lord, and we will look at it again tomorrow.

DAY 4

Begin by asking the Lord to speak to you through His Word today, and take a moment to review the memory verse for the week.

Let's pick up where we left off yesterday. We spent a moment glancing at a beautiful portrait of a man who trusted in the Lord his God. Who was it?

_____

Then we come face-to-face with those unbelieving Israelites, who we all too often resemble. They had seen miracle after miracle from the Lord in the desert, yet they did not trust in the Lord according to Deuteronomy 1:32. Let's find out why. Read Psalm 103 and take personally the love of God described there.

Now focus in on verse 7. According to the NIV, fill in the verse ...

> He made known his _____
> to Moses,
>
> (He made known) his _____
> to the people of Israel

God revealed His deeds to the people of Israel—through the miracles of parting the Red Sea, leading them with a cloud of fire and a cloud of smoke, by feeding them with manna and quail. He made His ways known to Moses. The Hebrew word translated "way" is the word *derek,* meaning journey, mode, manner, custom. It is used to demonstrate actions and behavior.[4]

God revealed the motives behind His action to Moses, while He only revealed the actions to the Israelites. That requires intimacy and closeness. Exodus 33 tells us about this intimacy between Moses and God.

Read Exodus 33:7–11. Who *could* inquire of the Lord?

_____

Who *did* inquire of the Lord?

_____

How did the Lord speak to him there?

_____

The Lord spoke to him as a man speaks to his friend. What closeness! "Friend" means what we would think it does—companion, neighbor, even husband; and this word is also used for one who is part of the family. Believers in Christ Jesus, who have received Him as their Lord and Savior are part of the family of God.

What does 1 John 3:1 call us?

_____

What a blessing beyond measure to be a part of the family of God, His own daughter! What is even more amazing is He does not leave it at a title, but He desires the relationship in its fullest meaning. He wants a face-to-face, intimate relationship with us. He knows us intimately; He made us according to Psalm 139. But we must seek to press in to know *Him* intimately.

Will you commit to knowing Him as He reveals Himself to us through His names over the next ten weeks? Write out a prayer of commitment to Him, pouring out an honest heart before Him.

_____

_____

_____

_____

_____

DAY 5

Begin by asking the Lord to speak to you through His Word today, and take a moment to review the memory verse for the week.

There are several verses throughout Scripture that mention or make reference to God's name. These passages can clue us further into the power, meaning, and significance of God's name as we prepare to dig into some of them specifically.

John 1:12 is one such powerful verse. Write it out below.

_____

_____

_____

_____

_____

_____

According to this verse, what do we need to believe in, in order to receive the right to be a child of God?

_____

In this verse, the word translated "name" is from the Greek *onoma*. It is a word meaning name, title, reputation; it is used for the person himself. *Onoma* is used to indicate the character described by the name, or identification with the person bearing the name. It is identified with the person's character and purpose. Keep that in mind as we study the names of God. His names are keeping with His character. If you want to know God, you study His names, simple as that.

With that in mind, read the promise in John 14:13. What does Jesus promise here?

_____

According to the definition of *onoma,* He will not just do what we ask of Him, but He will do whatever is in keeping with His character and purpose. What a blessing to know God is not the big genie in the sky, but rather a loving Father who does what is *best* for His children.

Now, read Matthew 6:9–13. Ask the Lord to let this passage fall afresh over you, even if you have read it a thousand times.

What does verse 9 say about His name?

_____

His name is to be hallowed, holy, and sacred. It is from the root word meaning "separated from ordinary." God's name is to be separated from the commonness of our world and our language. This was such a serious matter to the Jews that they would not dare utter His name or anything like it, but rather would refer to it as *Hashem,* meaning "the Name."

Even some modern day, English speaking Jews do not write the letters G-O-D. Do we have such reverence for the Lord in our own lives?

God the Father certainly makes Himself approachable through the blood of Jesus Christ. But that does not make Him any less holy or sacred than He was in the Old Testament. He is the same hallowed, sacred, and perfect God!

Read Psalm 20, concentrating on verses 7–8.

There are enemies out to destroy us. Satan, the devil, is our real and powerful enemy. The world we live in is certainly not helping us grow in godliness; on the contrary, we are either enemies with the world or enemies with God. (See James 4:4.) And unfortunately, our own flesh is not easily bowed to the truth and ways of God, making it an enemy of godliness as well.

These are powerful, destructive enemies. But according to Psalm 20:8, they are brought to their knees and fall while we rise up!

How is this so? According to verse 7, what do we have to put our trust in for us to have this victory?

When we put our trust and reliability in chariots and horses, in what we can see and touch, we will fall! We can get laid off, our health can weaken, and our family and friends can fail us. They are human. But the name (character, nature, and purpose) of our God will *never* fail us. On the contrary, trusting in it will cause us to rise up and stand firm.

My prayer as we embark on this journey of the names of God is that we will have such an intimate encounter with our God that we will forever be changed. I pray we would be awed, refreshed, and drawn to our knees by the power, majesty, and mercy of our Savior. Thank you for joining me on this adventure.

As you consider the reasons you have learned this week for studying God's names, would you respond in prayer to Him, and ask Him to give you the anticipation of knowing Him through His names?

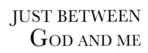

JUST BETWEEN
GOD AND ME

_____

_____

_____

_____

_____

_____

_____

_____

_____

_____

_____

_____

_____

_____

_____

_____

_____

_____

_____

_____

WHO IS ELOHIM?

The name "Elohim" is the plural form of the Hebrew word *El,* meaning god … either the One True God or false gods; the same word is used to refer to either. The name also carries the meaning of mighty and strong.[5] This is demonstrated in the use of this name throughout the account of creation in Genesis 1, as He makes everything from nothing. It also carries the meaning of creative, governing, omnipotence, and sovereignty as demonstrated in Hebrews 11:3.

If our God is monotheistic, one God, why does Scripture use the plural form of the word *El*? Our God reveals Himself in several instances as three in one—Father, Son, and Holy Spirit. He is one in essence and in nature, yet three distinct persons. We see examples of this in Deuteronomy 6:4, 32:39, and Isaiah 45:5, 22.

The principle of first mention is an important one in Scripture. It's the concept that at the first mention of a particular word in Scripture, God reveals much of the depth and definition associated with that word. Such is true for the names of God as well. The first mention of one of God's names is crucial to learning its meaning.

Elohim reveals Himself for the first time in His creation in Genesis 1. Of all His names, He chooses to open His Holy Word and the world introducing Himself as Elohim. The earth was formless and void as Elohim spoke over it for the first time (Genesis 1:2). That word brought light, life, and beauty to chaos. His Word is meant to bring healing life to all it affects (Psalm 107:20).

What portion of our own life needs healing? What area of our own hearts needs the application of His life-giving Word? Meditating on His Word and submerging ourselves in its truth will enable our broken, weary hearts to gain power and strength through healing like nothing else.

Ponder what God created—light, heaven, earth, and people. As we read through the creation account in Genesis, we see God created all things. As we encounter the creation of man, we see He chooses to use distinct words to describe this activity. First of all, in Genesis 1:26 we see that we are created in His image. This phrase is from the Hebrew word *selem,* meaning shadow of an original which lacks distinct characteristics of the original. We are created as the shadow of our Creator, yet we surely lack some distinct characteristics of Him. Praise Jesus that when He comes to dwell within our hearts, He fills us with His Spirit, as Ephesians 5 describes, which enables us to grow in our walk with Him and conforms our hearts into the image of His Son.

Three other distinct words are used to set apart the creation of mankind. The first is found in Genesis 1:26 and is translated "make" from the Hebrew *asah,* which literally means to do, to work, to make, create, accomplish, prepare. It is the fashioning of objects and it is used elsewhere in Scripture of God's creative activity (as in Psalm 86:9, 95:5, 96:5).[6] God made us from dirt, thus getting His holy hands dirty in the process. He expressed His perfect creativity in the creation of each one of us!

The second word used to describe the creation of mankind is found in Genesis 1:27 translated "created" from the Hebrew *bara,*—meaning to create, bring about, do, engrave, or carve.[7] What is distinct about this word is that it indicates a new creative act rather than a refashioning of an object; it signifies bringing into existence and refers only to an activity which can be performed by God. This word describes creation out of nothing. It is used in Psalm 51:10, where God creates within us a new, pure heart out of nothing. The newness is not in reference to time, but rather a reference to quality. God makes a *new* heart where our sinful one once was. At salvation, He makes you and me a new creation whether we are 10 or 110 years old. We are brand new in quality of purity and in reference to our rightness with God.

The final word used in the act of creating man is found in Genesis 2:7. It is a word translated "formed" from the Hebrew *yasar*—meaning to form, fashion, devise, produce, exist; it implies initiation, as well as structuring.[8] Isaiah 64:8 uses the same word to describe how God took the initiative to form His creation.

> Yet, O LORD, you are our Father. We are the clay, you are the potter; we are all the work of your hand.

It is a word that refers to being constructed *in advance*. This teaches us that God pre-thought about you *before* He ever created you! Jeremiah 29:11 tells us He knew the thoughts (or plans) He had for you. He made the plans while thinking the thoughts. There was purpose and pre-thought to your existence; *you* are not accidental ... regardless of the circumstances of your conception and birth. God had you in mind from before your conception.

So why did He create us? Why go through the trouble, since He foreknew the pain our sin would bring Him?

Consider Isaiah 43:1–13. God created us for a relationship with Him. He created us to glorify Him. All three of the "creation" words are used in verse 7. He created us for an intimate relationship with Him (v. 10). Three words here are used to identify that unique relationship:

- know (*yada*)—intimate and complete knowledge of each other, as a husband and wife know one another; used for sexual intimacy in marriage

- believe (*aman*)—to be firm, stable, established, firmly persuaded; used for "amen"

- understand (*bin*)—intelligent, process of perception and discernment[9]

Do we desire to know, believe, and understand Him as He desires to be known, believed, and understood? Let's pursue Him as He reveals Himself as Elohim through His Word this week.

MEMORY VERSE:

> For we are God's workmanship, created in Christ
> Jesus to do good works, which God prepared in
> advance for us to do.
>
> Ephesians 2:10

Begin by asking the Lord to speak to you through His
Word today, and then take a moment to write the new
memory verse on an index card. Remember to review
it often.

This week we are meeting God as our Elohim. He
chose to reveal Himself as such from the first line of
His Holy Word. "In the beginning, Elohim..."

He reveals Himself as the one who was before
time, and thus the eternal one who will always be. Yet
through the first chapter of Scripture, He continually
exposes Himself, the Creator, to the creation.

Begin by reading slowly through Genesis 1.

Then jot down all that He specifically creates according to this chapter.

_____

_____

_____

_____

_____

Elohim is used thirty-five times in the first two chapters of Scripture in connection with His power and might as revealed in creation. Why is it important in your life to know God as your Creator? Think back on the three techniques He used to create us.

_____

_____

_____

_____

_____

God creates with purpose. All that God does is purpose driven. He does nothing in vain. Look at a few examples in Scripture and write down what He does, and why He does it. What is His purpose, according to each passage below?

Isaiah 55:10–11

- What does God do here?

_____

_____

- Why does He do it?

_____

_____

Psalm 19:1–6

- What does God do here?

_____

- Why does He do it?

_____

1 Peter 2:9

- What does God do here?

_____

- Why does He do it?

_____

God always has a purpose in His activity. Therefore, when He chose to begin creation, He had an end product in mind. Not like the humanistic thinking where the earth is "godlike" in that it created everything on it through mindless, haphazard evolutions. God created you and I (and everything else) for *purpose,* far beyond what we can even comprehend. Most importantly, He made us for a relationship with Him. Not for us to just sit around in the midst of that relationship, but to *do* something with it.

Read Ephesians 2:8–10, and write out verse 10 below (it should look familiar):

_____

_____

_____

_____

What does this passage tell us we are created for in Christ Jesus?

_____

When did He prepare these good works for us?

_____

Before our conception, the Lord planned good works for each one of us, individually. Your "good works" may look different than my "good works," but most assuredly God has a plan and a calling on each one of our lives. What is the purpose of these good works?

Read Matthew 5:14–16, and finish the verse below:

... that they may see your _____ _____ and _____ your _____in heaven.

We are created to use our lives on this earth to point others to our Creator not just as a Creator, but as a Father, one in perfect, loving relationship with His children.

Take time this week to worship the Lord as your Elohim. You will dig into various aspects of this name each day; use that as a prompt to pray it back to Him for what it means to you in this season of life.

DAY 2

Begin by asking the Lord to speak to you through His Word today, and then take a moment to read the week's memory verse and practice saying it aloud, if possible.

As we studied yesterday, Elohim is our Creator God. There is an even more fascinating aspect to this truth.

Begin by reading back over Genesis 1. I know we have read it several times, but it carries more riches than Solomon ever had. Ask the Lord to give you fresh insight, and let the words fall on you as if you have never read them before. Try to visually *picture* what is happening.

Look specifically at verses 11–13. What exactly did God say? Write out His words from verse 11 below.

_____

_____

_____

Then what happened?

The _____ pro-
duced vegetation ... (v. 12a)

Do you see it? God not only works *on* creation, but He allows creation to work *with* Him. In one commentary it says,

For it is all of grace that Elohim should restore and
save His fallen creature. It is still greater grace that
in the restoration He makes that creature a fellow
worker with Himself.[10]

In His perfect grace, our God allows us to fellowship alongside Him.

What similar phrase do you find in 1 Corinthians 3:9
and 2 Corinthians 6:1–2? Write it here.

_____

What immeasurable grace our God, Elohim,
bestows on us that He would allow us to be fellow
workers with Him. It is His perfect way!

How can you and I come alongside our Elohim
and participate fully in His work? Meditate on the
directives of the following verses and write down what
they are telling you to do. Then apply them directly
to your life *right now.* How can you apply these in
your marriage, with your children, in your workplace,
in your church, in your neighborhood? Whatever
our spheres of influence, God desires us to apply His
truths there and thus become fellow workers.

John 13:34–35

_____

_____

_____

Hebrews 11:5–7

_____

_____

_____

1 Peter 3:1–6

_____

_____

_____

DAY 3

Begin by asking the Lord to speak to you through His Word today, and then take a moment to read the week's memory verse and practice saying it aloud, if possible.

As we study the names of God, we must understand in our finite minds that not only does our incredible God possess numerous names to capture every aspect of His greatness; but each of those names carries several qualities and attributes within it. What a multifaceted God we serve!

We have studied the creating element of Elohim, now we will dig a bit further and unveil another aspect. The word "Elohim" originally came from the Hebrew word, *alah*, which the Canaanites used for their false god, Baal. The word *alah* means to swear, and it describes one in covenant relationship with another.[11] Therefore, the name Elohim carries with it the promise of God's covenant making.

One thing we must understand about "covenant" is how it differs from "contract." When we form a contract with someone, we are in agreement providing the other person holds up his end of the bargain. When we purchase a home, we sign a contract. If the house is in the shape the contract outlines and the money is exchanged as the contract says, then the contract stands. If we stop paying the money to the bank for our house payments, then the contract ends, and the house is foreclosed.

Now, a covenant is quite a different matter. A covenant is based solely on the party who initiates it. In antiquity, a covenant was made in blood. The term "cutting covenant" began because the covenant was made when a sacrifice was cut in half and the one making covenant would pass through the pieces. One such covenant was the one God made with Abram (Genesis 15:8), which was amended after the exile through the prophets (Isaiah 42:6) and carried on through the Messiah (Malachi 3:1).

What does Hebrews 9:15 refer to Christ Jesus as? _____ of a _____ _____.

God has created a covenant of eternal life for those who will believe and place their faith in His Son.

Read Titus 1:1–3 and find out when He formed this covenant. Place a check by the correct answer according to verse 2.

_____ He formed it when He made us.
_____ He formed it at creation.
_____ He formed it before the beginning of time.

In the passage you just read, the name Elohim appears four times. Our Elohim is truly a covenant making God. Andrew Jukes states the following in his book *Names of God:*

The fact that God is Elohim, that is "the One who keepeth covenant," is the foundation of His creatures' hope in every extremity.[12]

What he is saying is that God's covenant with us is the very essence of our hope in Him. Without covenant, He could add and remove salvation according to our behavior. Instead, He commits Himself through covenant.

What happens to those who believe, according to Ephesians 1:13–14?

_____

Until when? (See Ephesians 4:30.)

_____

We are sealed by God, for covenant, until the day of our redemption in glory, when we are face-to-face with Him. Don't let the English word "until" trip you up, since it is not in reference to a time limit, but rather a word of promise. Essentially it is saying we are sealed in Him until we see Him in glory.

Close today as you read and meditate on the truth of Psalm 111:9.

DAY 4

Begin by asking the Lord to speak to you through His Word today, and then take a moment to read the week's memory verse and practice saying it aloud, if possible.

Our God is the same God from before time began until eternity. The one who reveals Himself as Elohim, revealed Himself in the same likeness through the earthly revelation of God in Jesus Christ (Colossians 1:15). Let's see the beautiful parallels of Scripture.

How does Genesis 1:1–2 describe the world prior to creation?

_____

What is the first thing God's presence introduces in verse 3?

_____

In the original language it just says, "God spoke, 'Light.' " The other words are added for clarity in English.

Now look at the reflection of Elohim in the New Testament. Read John 1:1–14. Who is the Word it is describing?

_____

What is "in Him", according to verse 4?

_____

And what is that life?

When we walk into a dark room, the first thing we do is flip on the light. Why? What does light do? Light dispels the darkness. The two cannot coexist.

In the beginning, God created light because it is foundational to everything else He created as a visual representation of His nature.[13] So how did Elohim create the world? What did He use? It was by the Word of His mouth (Psalm 33:6).

> In Hebrew thought, a word is the self-expression of a person. It comes from within him and it is him. By a word, you come into contact with the mind—the essential being—of the person who spoke it. The word is the hidden and invisible nature of the person brought out into the open. The unknown made known.[14]

Therefore, by Elohim speaking "Light," He reveals His essential nature to be light. Do we not find this to be so throughout the whole council of Scripture?

Write out James 1:17, and ponder its truth for a moment.

Scripture makes mention over and over to the power of light. We see this cord of "light" being woven throughout Scripture as a sign of the presence and nature of God Himself.

What does Jesus refer to Himself as in John 8:12?

_____

One commentary says this:

> Elohim is the Creator. At the beginning, He caused everything to be. Where there was nothing, He created everything. The Light of the world created sight in the eyes of a man who had never had sight. He did not restore sight—which implies that He would bring the man's eyes back to their original condition. He created sight where sight had never been.[15]

Even so, isn't light essential for sight? How much more so the light of Christ! He is not only light, but shines it for us.

Read Psalm 139:12, and fill in the verse:

> … even the darkness will not be dark to you; the night will _____ like the day for darkness is as _____ to you.

In the contrast of darkness, the light is its brightest. Have you ever left a dark movie theater in the middle of the day? You walk out into the bright parking lot, that was bright before you came in, but now it nearly blinds you! In the same way, in the midst of our own darkness of sin, loss, or suffering, His light shines its brightest. Are you willing to see it?

Okay, let's look at one more beautiful ray of light to encourage our weary souls. Read Philippians 2:14–16. What are we to be?

_____

How are we to do it?

When we let our Creator fill us with His love and His light each morning, we can walk through our day without complaining or arguing. We can then hold out the Word of life to this depraved world around us and shine like the stars our Creator cast into the heavens. Then we will know that we did not suffer in vain but for the great glory of our God!

Considering all you have learned this week about Elohim and now His parallel as the Light of the World, what does this mean to you? God is our Creator, who by nature has no darkness in Him, how does that minister to you as you seek to grow in relationship with Him?

_____

_____

_____

_____

_____

As you read these last few verses, ask the Lord to shed His light on them, and jot down their application to your life for this week.

Psalm 119:105

_____

_____

_____

_____

_____

Isaiah 9:2

_____

_____

_____

_____

_____

1 John 1:5–7

_____

_____

_____

_____

_____

DAY 5

Begin by asking the Lord to speak to you through His Word today, and then take a moment to read the week's memory verse and practice saying it aloud, if possible.

Today, let's wrap our week up by taking a hike up a mountain with the Light of the World. We have seen God as our Elohim, the Creator God, the covenant making God and the God who, without darkness, shines into the New Testament with clarity and purpose. Now, grab your sunglasses, and turn to Matthew 17:1–9. Read the passage carefully, visually picturing the scene.

Who went up the mountain?

_____

What happened there?

_____

_____

_____

When Jesus came into the world, He was cloaked with human flesh, which darkened the perfect light of God's being. On the mountain of transfiguration, God came unveiled before them, and what was revealed?

_____

What does this teach us about Him?

_____

_____

What does the truth of His "lightness" reveal about our own nature?

_____

_____

_____

A. W. Tozer has said,

Because we are the handiwork of God, it follows that all our problems and their solutions are theological. Some knowledge of what kind of God it is that operates the universe is indispensable to a sound philosophy of life and a sane outlook on the world scene. We can never know who or what we are till we know at least something of who God is. For this reason the self-existence of God is not a wisp of dry doctrine, academic and remote; it is in fact as near as our breath and as practical as the latest surgical technique. For reasons known only to Him, God honored man above all other beings by creating him in His own image. Man is a created being, a derived and contingent self, who of himself possesses nothing but is dependent each moment for his existence upon the One who created him after His own likeness. The fact of God is necessary to the fact of man.[16]

Have you found this to be true against the backdrop of this week's study? Jot down your thoughts.

_____

_____

_____

_____

Thinking on all you have studied this week, what truth will you carry with you? What has made the greatest impact on your own heart this week?

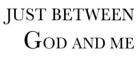

JUST BETWEEN
GOD AND ME

_____

_____

_____

_____

_____

_____

_____

_____

_____

_____

_____

_____

_____

_____

_____

_____

_____

_____

_____

_____

_____

WHO IS YAHWEH?

One of the most common names we use to refer to God in the English language is "Lord." One of the original words translated "Lord" is the holiest name for God, Yahweh. Yahweh comes from the Hebrew *tetragrammatron* (meaning four letters) YHWH. There are no vowels that translate from the Hebrew language to the English language. The name "Yahweh" is represented in the English Bible by the capital letters LORD. The Hebrew language is closer in appearance to Chinese or Egyptian than to English, in that is it written with symbols rather than letters. When it is translated to English, it is obviously represented in letters. This is why the correct transliteration for this name of God is "YHWH."

Each of the four letters used to spell out this personal name of God (YHWH or more correctly YHVH, since the Hebrew language has no equivalent to *w*) represents a different symbol which uniquely points to the Trinity.

The first letter *Y* is from the Hebrew letter whose symbol represents a closed fist. This is indicative of power and ownership, and it points us to the Father God.

The Hebrew letter translated *H* is the letter whose symbol means to "behold" or "reveal," and it is indicative of gentleness and represents the Holy Spirit of God. This is the letter God used in Genesis 17 to add to Abram's name, making it Abraham. This example demonstrates God breathing His life-giving Spirit into a man as He did at Creation, but even more fascinating, it points us on to the New Testament where God breathes His Spirit into each new believer.

Finally, the letter translated *V* or *W* in the English is from the Hebrew letter that symbolizes a nail or being bound.[17] This is clearly a picture of the Son of God, Jesus Christ. Isn't it fascinating how God reveals Himself as a Trinity? It is even evident in the nailed Son from as early as Genesis chapter 2, which was thousands of years before Roman crucifixion came into existence.

In order to derive a definition for an unfamiliar word in Hebrew, they often look to other words that may appear similar. Therefore, Hebrew words associated with Yahweh are the words *havah*, meaning *to be* and *chavah* meaning *to live* or *life*.[18] Thus, when God displays Himself as YHWH, He is pronouncing His existence, or the one who causes existence. It is the idea of being fully independent—absolutely self-existent.

This name is also rendered "I AM" in the English Bible, which conveys that God is not only self-existent, but always in the present with His people. This is the most common definition for this name of God. The name occurs over 6, 800 times in the Old Testament alone, and it appears in every book of the Bible except Esther, Song of Solomon, and Ecclesiastes.

This name of God was once spoken by priests worshiping in the Jerusalem temple. After the destruction of the temple in 70 AD, the name's pronunciation was lost. Adonay was substituted in the biblical texts, thus losing the correct pronunciation of the name. Eventually, the vowels of the Hebrew "Adonay" were integrated into "YHWH," forming "Yahweh," which was first rendered "Jehovah" in the middle ages, originating from the German pronunciation.

God first reveals Himself as Yahweh in Genesis 2:4–9 in connection to Elohim. The first occurrence is in direct relation to man. Elohim is concerned with creation as a whole and creating man in relationship to Him. Yahweh is concerned with man enjoying God, and therefore placing him under moral obligations with warnings for punishment and disobedience.

It is interesting that in the account of Genesis 3:1–7, where Satan visits Eve in order to deceive her, there is no mention of Yahweh. This could be that even Satan in the midst of his evil and sin, cannot acknowledge Yahweh because of His holiness. But in verse 8, Yahweh is the One who calls Adam and Eve to account for their sin.

Yet He never acts apart from His love, as demonstrated in Genesis 7:1–6, 16. Even in regards to the building of the ark, Elohim is in reference to saving the creation in the ark; but Yahweh in verse 5 is making a way of restoration with man and pronounces judgment.

So how does knowing we serve a holy and just God affect us? Romans 3:23 clearly teaches that we have all fallen short of His perfection. In this, God reveals to us our own desperate need for a Savior, for eternal life. He answers to that need even as He utters it, because Yahweh *is* life, the very life we lack!

DAY 1

MEMORY VERSE:

> Be still before the LORD and wait patiently for Him; do not fret when men succeed in their ways, when they carry out their wicked schemes.
>
> Psalm 37:7 (NIV)

Begin in prayer, asking the Lord to speak to you through His Word. Remember to make a note card with your memory verse this week, and practice it often.

What a deep name of God we are studying this week! We really can only begin to scratch the surface of *any* of these names, especially Yahweh. Many scholars devote their entire lives to in-depth study of God's Word, including His names. Yet these men die—never having reached the bottom of all its riches.

The name Yahweh has carried a mystery through the ages. The true name and pronunciation is forever lost, since the desecration of the temple at Jerusalem.

Do you remember what the characters of the Hebrew letters represent?

_____

Fascinating, isn't it? What a complex and in-depth God we serve!

I want you to keep all of this in mind as we seek to uncover some of the truth behind this most commonly noted name in Scripture. We will not get to the bottom of it, but if we seek to find Him and hear from Him in the midst of our search, He will show up (Jeremiah 29:13–14).

The most overriding aspect of this name of God is found in Psalm 103:1. Read the entire psalm slowly and prayerfully. It is a masterpiece!

This psalm gives such a rich depth to describing who Yahweh is and what He does for you and me. According to verse 1, what is the overriding characteristic represented in Yahweh?

God's character contains numerous virtues, but above all else our God is holy. The word "holy" has lost much of its significance and meaning in our Christian circles. The Hebrew word here is *Qodes*, and it means to consecrate. The root of this word means to pronounce clean, to sanctify, and purify; it denotes something that is withheld from ordinary use and treated with special care. God is separate from all evil, death, idolatry, and imperfections.

We, on the other hand, are submerged and filled with much evil, living in the shadow of death and surrounded by idol worship; in particular money, TV, and even self. You don't have to know yourself too well to know you are imperfect! But we were not made for this fallen world and this fallen state of living. Our souls cry out for holiness, purity, perfection, goodness, and life.

The psalmist here in Psalm 103 is consoling his soul with the praise of what is holy and perfect, Yahweh. The psalmist is causing his soul to remember the benefits of Yahweh and what a holy God does for His fallen and desperately needy child. Are you in need of a huge, holy, capable God? I know I am! Let's remind our souls of all His benefits. List the benefits below, according to verses 2–5.

_____

_____

_____

_____

I don't know about you, but I have certainly had need for all of these at one time or another, sometimes all at once. Do you need forgiveness, healing, redemption from a pit, love and compassion, or a pure satisfaction for your desires? Praise Yahweh for being enough for all of these benefits!

Which of these benefits speaks most directly into a need in your life right now? And why?

_____

_____

_____

_____

_____

Your God, your LORD, Yahweh is enough for that need. Pour out your heart to Him, and seek His filling.

Now spend a moment reading Psalm 103 again, and jot down the verbs following the word LORD. I'll give you an example of what I mean:

The LORD *works righteousness.* (v. 6)

The LORD _____.

The LORD _____.
The LORD _____.

The LORD _____.

The LORD _____.
The LORD _____.

The LORD _____.

The LORD _____.
The LORD _____.

All the verbs you wrote describe truth about who our Yahweh is. He is working righteousness, making known His deeds and ways; He is compassionate, gracious, and slow to anger and so much more!

None of the names of God in Scripture are used out of context. Every name He chooses to use in a particular setting, chapter, or situation in Scripture is the perfect revelation of God in that instance. Therefore, in Psalm 103, with all its colorful brushstrokes of forgiveness, healing, and compassion, our holy God steps in and says, "I am Yahweh of that situation in you!" He is our forgiveness, healing, and compassion and all the verbs you wrote.

Meditate on all of who the Lord is in the midst of all your pain, difficulties, needs, failures, and emptiness. Pour out your heart to Him.

DAY 2

· ·

Begin in prayer, asking the Lord to speak to you through His Word. Remember to practice your memory verse before starting your study time today.

What was the overriding characteristic we learned about our Yahweh yesterday?

_____

Now let's dig into *our response* to His holiness. Moses was called by God to lead the people of Israel out of Egypt. As they came up against the Rea Sea, God chose to reveal His glory by parting it for the Israelites and drowning their enemies in it. How would you respond?

How did Moses respond? Read Moses' response in Exodus 15:1–18. Remember that where you see "God" in the passage it's the name "Elohim" (Creator, light-shining, covenant-making God) and where you see "Lord" it is "Yahweh."

Moses knew the holiness of his Lord. Write out verse 3 below:

_____

_____

_____

Do you need someone to fight for you? Someone to uphold your cause? Someone to vindicate you? Yahweh is a warrior!

What does verse 11 say about Him?

_____

_____

In response to a miracle, Moses recognized and acknowledged Yahweh's holiness. Where did Moses pray the Lord would guide them to?

_____

Moses not only recognized the holiness of God, but prayed to be guided to His holy dwelling as well. As I said before, our souls yearn for holiness. Just as Moses responded with a desire for holiness after encountering the LORD's holiness, we ought to press ourselves against the backdrop of His holiness and seek to grow in it ourselves.

Write down the common denominator of each of the following verses:

Leviticus 19:1–2

_____

Leviticus 20:26

_____

1 Thessalonians 4:7

_____

1 Peter 1:15–16

Yahweh created man to enjoy and exhibit His righteousness—so He demands righteousness, justice, and holiness from the creatures made in His image. Yahweh, the Holy One, has called you and me to live holy lives—free from impurity and sin. As children of God, we have put off our sinful nature and taken up a new man of purity. But as humans in a fallen world, we stumble constantly. So how do we live pure, holy, and blameless? Is it even possible? Well, would God call us to something we can't achieve?

Read Psalm 19:12–13. The psalmist says *then* I will be blameless. When will he be blameless? He is blameless when he is kept, by the power of God working in him, from willful sins.

As believers living this side of glory, we will never reach a perfect state of sinlessness. Only Jesus was fully human and fully sinless because He was fully divine. But, by the power of the Holy Spirit working within us, we can get to where we are not *planning* sin. We are not *willfully* sinning.

When we meditate on our husband's wrongs after he leaves for work, and we decide we will "get him" when he gets home, we are planning sin. When our boss makes us nuts and we decide to get even, we are planning sin. When that good-looking guy is giving us more attention than our man is lately and we allow even our thoughts to flirt with disaster, we are planning sin. When we take our sinful thoughts to the

Lord *before* we act on them and ask Him to purify our hearts giving us the strength to walk in righteousness, then we are blameless before Him. By allowing God to purge sin from our heart, he is freeing us of willful sin. Then we are blameless before him.

We can be free of all willful sin. But we must be willing to be radical with our purging of sin, this includes getting professional help, if needed.

Is there anything in your life the Lord wants to purge so you can walk blamelessly before Him?

Read Psalm 19:14. Pray it back to Yahweh, and ask Him to redeem you through and through. He promises to do it! (See 1 Thessalonians 5:23–24.)

To personalize that last verse in 1 Thessalonians: The one who calls me is faithful, and He will do it. What does Psalm 138:8 say about Yahweh?

Spend some time meditating on the truths you've learned today, and take a moment to praise your Redeemer, Yahweh.

DAY 3

Begin in prayer, asking the Lord to speak to you through His Word. Remember to practice your memory verse before starting your study time today.

As we have studied the name of Yahweh, we have seen a glimpse of God's holiness and how He calls us to holiness. Yahweh is holy, judging sin, yet redeeming and delivering His people. Let's look at one instance where this perfect God first introduced Himself to a humble shepherd.

As you read the passage, notice the various names used for God. Read Exodus 3:1–6.

Elohim, the relationship heart of God, the covenant *maker*, pursued Moses. Now see how Yahweh, the covenant *keeper* who judges sin, calls Moses to a task of carrying out His covenant and judging sin in verses 7–12.

What does Elohim promise Moses in verse 12?

_____

Do you see the relationship heart of Elohim? Then Moses asks something curious of God in verse 13, what is it?

_____

In *Trusting in the Names of God,* the author makes this observation:

God called Moses to a monumental task requiring enormous trust. Moses' first question of God was related to His character. Moses wanted to know who God was and asked a bold and courageous question of God. He asked God what he should say if the people asked, "What is His name?" What a good question. And oh, what an answer God gave to Moses that day.[19]

Let's look at God's answer (read verses 14–17):

Who did He say He was:

_____

What did He say He does:

_____

The same commentary says of this passage,

When God revealed His name, I AM WHO I AM, He spoke His name using Hebrew verbs, not nouns. The verb forms are imperfect tense, implying continuing, unfinished action: "I am the one who always is."[20]

God revealed Himself as Yahweh to Moses. Moses was wise to seek to know God, in order to trust Him. Do you trust God? I mean _really_ trust Him? It's not easy, especially without a burning bush! We must trust on faith alone. What did Jesus say about that? Read John 20:29.

_____

The same Yahweh who called the Israelites out of their bondage, calls you and me out of ours. Now look up and write out Psalm 3:8 below.

_____

_____

_____

_____

In yesterday's lesson we looked at some areas where we may be held by a ruling sin or a sin that keeps us in bondage. Yahweh offers deliverance. When we place our trust in Jesus, we are released from the bondage of death. But as we grow in our walk, we are released from bondages to our past, to bitterness and pride. God does not just desire your salvation, He desires you to live a life of freedom. Look up and meditate on Galatians 5:1.

Is there an area of your heart that is in bondage? Are you harboring bitterness against someone who has hurt you? Are you carrying a burden of a sin you feel is unforgiven? Do you live out life protecting yourself with pride and selfishness because you don't yet know your God is for you? You and I do not have to look out for ourselves because a very mighty Yahweh is looking out for our best interest.

Ask the Lord to show you verses to memorize, and renew your mind on any area where He is revealing you are in bondage. A concordance is a wonderful tool for this.

DAY 4

Begin in prayer, asking the Lord to speak to you through His Word. Remember to practice your memory verse before starting your study time today.

As we have considered the truths of the holiness and judgment of Yahweh, we can't help but come face-to-face with our own depravity of soul and our own sinfulness. We cannot even *attempt* to be made right before God on our own. Yahweh proves that to us over and over. He must judge sin. It is His holy nature. So what is fallen man to do?

Well, to His great glory, He has made a way through Jesus. The very name of Jesus speaks promise and covenant from a holy Yahweh. Read Matthew 1:21, and write below why He was to be named "Jesus."

_____

_____

And save them He did! The name Jesus in Hebrew is "Yeshuam", and it literally means "Yahweh saves" or "Yahweh is salvation." What a glorious name it is. When did He save us and from what?

Read Romans 5:6–8.

_____

_____

_____

The name Yeshua, Jesus (in English) or Iesous (in Greek), is a contraction of the Hebrew name Yeshoshua, translated "Joshua" in some English Bibles. The name Joshua is the oldest name containing Yahweh, the covenant name of God. Yeshua is also related to the word *yeshu'ah,* which means salvation.

Read Acts 4:12. To what name is this verse referring?

_____

When you hear the name Jesus what do *you* think of?

_____

_____

_____

Jesus was a common name in first-century Palestine. Its popularity was mostly due to the fact that they knew the meaning of Yeshua and so desired Yahweh's salvation over their children. Oh, but how sad that most of the Jews missed it!

In their monotheistic minds, God could not be a man because the Lord is one (Deuteronomy 6:4). God is deity so how could He be man like them? Perplexing. What a glorious God who would come as fully man and fully God to redeem a people lost in sin. Based on all of this, why do you think He sent an angel to Joseph to announce the birth of Jesus? Read Matthew 1:18–25.

_____

_____

_____

Why do you think Jesus' name paralleled the covenant-keeping name of God? What is the significance of who Jesus proved Himself to be?

Read Exodus 24:4–8 and 1 Peter 1:18–20 and Revelation 1:5.

_____

_____

_____

_____

_____

_____

_____

Close in prayer to the Yahweh who sent Jesus just for you.

DAY 5

Begin in prayer, asking the Lord to speak to you through His Word. Then spend a moment practicing your memory verse.

God is so near us when we pursue Him through His Word. Today, spend time in the encouragement of the promises found in Jesus. First of all, do you remember what "Jesus" means?

_____

If you did not remember, glance back at yesterday's study, and let the truth of it soak into your soul. Now, let's absorb some of those promises based on His name. For each one, write the significance of the name of Jesus based on that passage.

Acts 16:31

_____

_____

_____

_____

1 Corinthians 6:11

_____

_____

_____

_____

Philippians 2:9–11

_____

_____

_____

_____

Colossians 3:17

_____

_____

_____

_____

Hebrews 12:1–2

_____

_____

_____

_____

Which one did you find the most significant in your season of life right now? Why?

_____

_____

_____

_____

_____

What an incredible God we serve! Do you see it more and more as we dig into each aspect of His nature? What has been the most profound truth for you this week as we have met Yahweh?

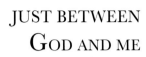

JUST BETWEEN
GOD AND ME

_____

_____

_____

_____

_____

_____

_____

_____

_____

_____

_____

_____

_____

_____

_____

_____

_____

_____

_____

_____

_____

_____

WHO IS ADONAI?

What comes to mind when you think of being mastered? Does slavery come to mind? What about an image of bondage and chains?

The one true living God desires to be our Master, but the irony in it is that His mastery breaks us free of bondage and the chains of sin.

The Hebrew word *adonai* refers to "lord" or "master." It is the plural form of *adon* and is usually in reference to our God as our personal Lord and Master. The word is written in our English Bibles as "Lord" when referring to the one true God. But the word can refer to people as well. The literal translation is a possessive term "my lord's."[21] The lordship of God means His total possession of me and my total submission to Him as Lord and Master.

Adonai is a name that *completely* depicts relationship. The title can appear in conjunction with Yahweh, where as it is then depicted as "Sovereign Lord" or "Lord God" in some English translations.

In Genesis 15:2, the Lord first reveals Himself as Adonai through His relationship with Abram. Slavery was common and well known during that time. When Abram calls Yahweh his Adonai, it is an outpouring of the realization of his own inadequacy, frailty, and total dependence upon God.

Servants were totally dependent upon their masters for all of their needs. It was the master's responsibility to care for and protect his slaves. The master even provided direction in the slave's day-to-day living. Therefore, for Abram to acknowledge God as his Master, he was claiming that dependence upon Him. Is this how you and I are living in our own relationship with God? Do we realize how dependent we really are? How would we live differently if we did?

Many people seem almost disappointed with Christianity. It doesn't seem to satisfy them as they had envisioned, so they give themselves to worldly, temporal temptations. But have you ever wondered if it is that Christianity does not satisfy or could it be that they have never experienced Christianity as Christ intended?

How many people really live out Philippians 1:20–21? Our commitment to His will ought to be the norm, not the exception. Are you and I living out our servitude and obedience?

As I pondered this, it occurred to me that God has the *right* to expect obedience. Consider the account in Exodus 4:10–14. Why was God angry? Isn't it because Moses was saying to Him, "Lord, Lord," but he was not trusting and fully submitting to His authority as Adonai?

So what about you? How will you live out your obedience to the Lord and Master of your life? What is interesting is that we are living in obedience to a master ... whether that master is "self," sin, the world, approval of others, our past. We are bowing down to a master and serving his way whether we like it or not. How can we tell who we are serving? A quick check of the fruit we are bearing is a good indication of our master. Are we bearing fruitful, Christ-centered lives? Or do we need to reconsider to whom we have given the title of "Lord"?

DAY 1

· ·

MEMORY VERSE:

> Therefore everyone who hears these words of mine
> and puts them into practice is like a wise man who
> built his house on the rock.
>
> Matthew 7:24

Begin in prayer asking the Lord to open your eyes
to see wonderful truths in His Word today. Spend a
moment reviewing the memory verse for the week.
Remember to jot it down on an index card to practice
throughout the week.

As we embark on digging into Adonai and the
truths hidden under the surface, let's pray for obedient hearts. Remember, Jesus is not looking to just hear
"Lord, Lord," but to see us put feet to our words.

As we learned in the introduction, the overriding
meaning of Adonai calls out the "lordness" of God.
He is Lord and Master of those who are willing to
submit to being His very dependent servants. Let's try
to uncover a bit more of the depth of this truth and
see how we can live it out in our lives.

As Americans, we can live sheltered lives from
what true servitude is. The Lord Jesus gave an example of what a true humble servant looks like in Luke
17:7–10. Read the passage carefully. Then fill in the
last verse.

So you also, when you have done _____
_____ you were
_____ to do, should say, "We are
_____ servants; we have only
done our duty."

Does it bristle up against you as it does me? Servitude is very misconstrued in our culture. Consider this quote from *Praying the Names of God:*

> "Servant" is not a particularly popular word in our culture. It sounds demeaning, belittling, hardly something we should aspire to. Such an attitude can make it hard for us to understand our position as servants of the Lord. Perhaps that's why we so often get things reversed, treating God as though He were some kind of celestial butler who should use His divine power to further our plans. With that kind of attitude underlying our prayers, it is a wonder the Lord answers so many of them. Perhaps it is time to repent and ask God to help us to give Him the kind of perfect service that Jesus Himself did.[22]

Humbling, isn't it? How I pray my heart would be that of a true servant before her Master.

Let's look at a biblical example of a servant called by God in Scripture. Read Judges 6:11–16. Remember where you see "LORD," it's referring to Yahweh; where you see "Lord," its referring to Adon or Adonai.

Who initiated this encounter?

_____

Most scholars agree, in the Old Testament, where you often find "the angel of the Lord," it is referring to a pre-incarnate Christ. So you can interpret this passage to read that God Himself showed up and initiated this interaction with Gideon.

What is the first thing the Lord says to Gideon (v. 12)?

_____

_____

What is Gideon's response?

_____

_____

Gideon uses the word "Adon" to address this mysterious man who has appeared to him. It was a term of respect used at the time. He is not yet acknowledging God's Lordship. He is still questioning the presence of God. Gideon wants certainty and clarity that he stands before his God. He builds an altar of sacrifice and God essentially "proves" Himself there to Gideon. Now read Gideon's response to knowing he is in God's presence in verse 22. What does Gideon call Him?

_____

He acknowledges God's holiness and covenant keeping sovereignty and he bows himself as servant before Him, recognizing who the Master is by using both names, Yahweh and Adonai. Through the episode, God goes on to place a call on Gideon's life and gives him a miraculous victory. As His servants, we can count on gaining the victory as we stay near our Master.

Gideon's story reminds me of one of my favorite women in all of Scripture, known as the Proverbs 31 woman. She is described in Proverbs 31:10–31.

The name God calls Gideon in Judges 6:13 "mighty warrior" is the same word translated "noble character" in Proverbs 31:10. This was a mighty warrior woman!

What was her attitude, according to Proverbs 31:13?

She worked with _____ hands.

This is a woman with a yes-heart attitude toward what God called her to do. Why did she have this attitude? See verse 30.

_____

The word in the NIV translated "fear" is a word meaning reverence and awe. This woman eagerly or willingly worked at what the Lord had given her to do because she respected her Master. Her "Master" was not her husband, her boss, or (Lord help us!) her children. She understood her Master was Yahweh. She had a right heart, so her attitude followed.

Read Luke 6:43–45. According to this verse, what comes from our mouth is from our _____.
Notice what Jesus immediately follows this teaching with.

Living out Adonai as our Master and Lord begins with our heart. It is a heart issue. Is your heart fully and radically surrendered to Adonai? If not, what is hindering you?

_____

_____

_____

Acknowledging God as our Adonai is also an issue of trust. The slaves had to fully trust their masters had their best interest in mind. Certainly some did not. What did Jesus say in Mark 10:18?

_____

Yes, Jesus is God and Jesus is good. He was testing the rich man He was speaking to those who did not believe Jesus was fully God. But our lesson in this study is that God alone is good. We can trust Him as Master because He is good always. His judgments are good, His plan is good, His ways are good, and He works out good in our lives (Romans 8:28). Are we fully believing this with our actions?

What are your hesitations and fears about trusting Adonai as your Master. He already knows, but as we lay it out before Him, He will apply His truth.

Begin in prayer asking the Lord to open your eyes to see wonderful truths in His Word today. Spend a moment reviewing the memory verse for the week.

What does the world view as "great" or "powerful"? List a few things:

_____

_____

Now, let's compare that with biblical greatness. In Matthew 20: 26–28, what does Jesus say greatness is?

_____

_____

_____

Polar opposites, aren't they? According to verse 27, what does the one who wants to be first have to be?

_____

What did the Son of Man come to do, according to this passage?

_____

_____

Are you and I looking for who we can serve, or are we looking to be served? Before we answer too quickly think on this, am I frustrated when I have to pick up my husband's socks for the tenth time today? Do I get short-tempered with my children when they interrupt my "me" time? Am I willing to joyfully cook a meal for a neighbor in need or serve in the church nursery, even though I don't "feel" like it today? Do I live for "me"?

I would love to say I am looking to be a servant like Jesus describes, with a willing heart. Unfortunately, I all too often seek out to serve self rather than deny self. What about you?

_____

_____

_____

_____

Jesus gave us beautiful examples of servitude over and over in the Scripture. Let's look at a couple.

Read Matthew 14:1–21. It is several verses, but try to envision the scene. What would you have done in Jesus' shoes?

_____

_____

He had been through enough, the beheading of His cousin and friend, trying to take a few minutes with the Father to grieve, and here come the crowds.

And not just any crowd, a crowd with needs—sick people, disabled people, dying people, possessed people. Imagine the noise, the smells, and the depth of depravity closing in around Him, as His soul mourns for John. Jesus was fully man and fully God. He *felt* emotion, grief, and pain. He grew tired, weary, and hungry.

I get grumpy if my quiet time in the morning is interrupted too early, so I cannot fathom trying to get alone with the Father over such grief and being bombarded with the needs of others.

What did Jesus do according to verse 14?

_____

_____

In the midst of the deep needs of His own soul, He chose to deny self and serve others with compassion. Oh, to be like Jesus! Don't miss what happened as this already long day grew longer. Read verses 15–16 again. What time of day is it?

_____

And yet, our Savior chooses to serve again. What a model for us! What a Master we serve that He denies Himself for our sakes, out of compassionate love.

How can we mimic His example of servitude in our own lives as we live out our service to our Master Jesus? Give practical examples of what you can do this week to serve like Jesus.

_____

_____

_____

_____

_____

_____

_____

_____

We cannot do it apart from Him, though. Spend a moment prayerfully asking Him to empower you to let your light shine this week so that others will see your good deeds and glorify your Father in heaven (Matthew 5:16).

DAY 3

Begin in prayer asking the Lord to open your eyes to see wonderful truths in His Word today. Spend a moment reviewing the memory verse for the week.

Today, let's look at another example where Jesus was a model servant for us to mimic. Read John 13:1–5.

What did Jesus do in this instance that demonstrated His servitude?

_____

_____

_____

People of the time wore open leather shoes as they walked from town to town. Their feet would become caked with mud, dust, and even blood as their feet calloused in the primitive shoes. Servants in each home would clean the feet of those who came in order to show hospitality on behalf of the master of the house. Notice it was still their *servant* who did the cleaning though.

Jesus Himself took on the filth of those disciples' feet onto the towel He had tied to His waist. What a foreshadowing picture of taking our filthy sins on Himself. How was Jesus able to kneel on the floor before these men—one of which would turn Him in to the authorities and result in His death—and clean their filthy feet with His own hands?

Write out the first part of verse 3:

Jesus _____ the Father had
put _____ things under
his power, and that he had _____
_____ _____ and was
_____ to God.

Jesus did not have low-self esteem issues. He knew who He was, whose He was, and where He was going! Therefore, He could compassionately, willingly, and joyfully serve those around Him. He had nothing to prove to them. He did not live His life wondering what others thought; He lived His life in pure servitude to the will of the Father.

Write out Galatians 1:10 from your Bible:

_____

_____

_____

_____

We cannot live as a true bondservant to Christ and still be serving the world through our addictions, our time, our money, and our concern about pleasing men.

Just as Jesus, we have got to know and believe who we are, whose we are, and where we are headed!

Who are you? Write down your initial thoughts:

_____

_____

In God's economy, you are not defined by the name your parents' gave you, by the economic status you hold, by the job you do, or by the people you are related to—except One.

Read 1 John 3:1, and write down what it says you are— if you have placed your reliance on Jesus Christ as your Savior.

I am

_____

Do you believe it? Does your life reflect it? I have this quote written in the front of my Bible, "Faith is not what you *say* you believe—but what you are *really living* out!" Not really sure where I heard it, but I have definitely found it to be true.

Whose are you? The very nature of this study is to uncover the answer to that very question. As we get to know whose we are and who He is—His nature, character, and heart—we will grow in our confidence of not having to live for the approval of men but for the pleasure of the God we serve. Over the last four weeks, you have studied some of the names of God and His character. At this point you can answer a bit about whose you are. Whose are you? Who is your God?

_____

_____

_____

Once we know a bit of who we are and whose we are, we are wise to follow the example of the psalmist in Psalm 123:1–2. What did that slave do?

_____

The personal slaves and the maidservants of the past would fix their eyes on the hands of their master and anticipate every move. They would be ready to serve their master as soon as the master moved. Are our eyes so fixed on our Master, as a maidservant's are on hers, that we anticipate His every move?

The last part of John 13:3 illustrates how well Jesus knew where He was headed. According to this verse, where was He headed?

_____

Where are you headed? For those who have trusted Christ Jesus as their personal Lord (Adonai) and Savior, you can read the following passages about where you are headed. For each passage, take note of how it is described.

John 14:1–4

_____

Luke 23:43

_____

Mark 10:21

_____

Mark 16:19

_____

Philippians 1:21

_____

Revelation 4

_____

What if we lived as if we believed this was true? How would we behave, speak, and serve? Could we have humility here knowing the reality is we are daughters of the King of the universe, headed for a heavenly kingdom? We have nothing to prove to those here, but we are freed up to live in complete service to the one who is our life.

Spend time sharing your heart with your loving Master and asking Him for a right perspective and Christ-like heart from which to serve.

DAY 4

Begin in prayer asking the Lord to open your eyes to see wonderful truths in His Word today. Spend a moment reviewing the memory verse for the week.

We have been getting to know God as our Adonai, our Lord, and our Master. In light of what we have learned this week, what is your understanding of "Adonai"?

_____

_____

What does God's lordship mean to you in your personal life during this season?

_____

_____

_____

In the New Testament, Jesus is clearly depicted as Adonai, as well. The Greek word (remember "Adonai" is Hebrew) is *Kurios,* meaning supreme in authority and control. It is the word most commonly used in reference to Jesus Christ. The other word used often to denote "lord" in the Greek is *despotes,* which means absolute ruler.[23] Both are used often of Jesus. As our Master, He has expectations of His servants. Remember, we don't want to say "Lord, Lord" and not mean it with our lives.

In the following passages, make note of how Jesus is depicted as Adonai and what is required of us.

Luke 14:25–27

_____

_____

_____

Matthew 10:34–40

_____

_____

_____

Romans 10:8–10

_____

_____

_____

Let us not deceive ourselves, ladies, we *are* slaves whether we like it or not. What does 2 Peter 2:19 say we are slaves to?

_____

Therefore we can either be mastered by our sin (John 8:34) or by our God. How does Romans 6:15–18 illustrate this theology? In other words, how does the passage in Romans highlight what we are talking about?

_____

_____

_____

_____

_____

_____

Read on in verse 19 and fill it in below:

> … you are _____ in your
> natural selves … you used to offer the parts of
> your body in _____
> to _____ and to ever-
> increasing _____, so now
> offer them in _____ to
> _____ leading to
> _____.

I don't know about you, but I can certainly attest to having offered parts of my body as a slave to impurity and wickedness. He can redeem those parts and purify my heart and soul so I can offer my body in slavery to righteousness which leads to holiness. I can serve my family, joyfully submit to my man, wash clothes, make dinners, home school my children, cook meals for neighbors, give of my time, talents, and money in order to further the kingdom of God. All because I am a slave moving on to holiness.

What about you? Can you attest to having lived a life of impurity and wickedness? Have you seen a change in your life as you have sought to live as a slave to righteousness? Write your thoughts to your Adonai.

_____

_____

_____

DAY 5

Begin in prayer asking the Lord to open your eyes to see wonderful truths in His Word today. Spend a moment reviewing the memory verse for the week.

As we conclude our week with Adonai, let's review some of the virtues this name of God encompasses. List as many as you can think of and flip through the week to jog your memory.

_____

_____

_____

Living as a slave to this world and to sin leads to death. Living as a slave to Adonai and to righteousness leads to life. Let's relish some of the blessings of living sacrificially for our Adonai. Read each of the following passages and make note of the blessing of those willing to be humble, lowly servants.

Ezekiel 21:26

_____

Matthew 23:12

_____

John 12:25–26

_____

1 Peter 5:5–7

_____

What benefits of being a slave of righteousness!

Another incredible blessing of living in servitude to our Master is found in Galatians 2:20. What comfort for our souls is found in this verse?

_____

Is not the most primitive need of a person to be unconditionally loved and cared for by someone?

How much does this Galatians verse say Christ loves you and me?

_____

Finally, let's look at a passage rich with treasure, Ephesians 1:4–14. It is overflowing with the truth of our blessings in Christ Jesus. Take a moment, and read through this passage slowly, absorbing the truths laid out here. Write down all that it says you are: (Here's an example.)

I am _chosen (v. 4)_

I am _____

I am _____

I am _____

I am _____

I am _____

I am _____

I am _____

Spend some time journaling what the Lord has taught you this week.

JUST BETWEEN
GOD AND ME

_____

_____

_____

_____

_____

_____

_____

_____

_____

_____

_____

_____

_____

_____

_____

_____

_____

_____

_____

_____

_____

WHO IS EL SHADDAI?

The Lord, in His perfect provision, created each one of us with very specific needs that we will seek to fill in any way possible. Having empty places within our souls is not comfortable. God knows that. He provides the perfect filler for our souls in Himself. The next name we will study beautifully conveys this truth.

El Shaddai is a two-part name. The first part *El* is the singular word for god. You might remember the plural we studied a few weeks ago, Elohim. The word El can refer to the one true God or to a false god, idol, or deity. The word also carries the connotation of strong or mighty.

The second part of this name is *Shaddai.* Many believe this also means strong or even powerful, and it occurs forty-eight times in the Old Testament translated "Almighty." But the root word (*shad*), from which Shaddai is derived, is translated several times in Scripture as "breast."

Therefore, the most in-context meaning for "Shaddai" would be one who nourishes, supplies, and satisfies. There is definitely power associated with the breast though. Any nursing mother would agree. The breast can quiet, comfort, and relax a tired or hungry baby, in the same way El Shaddai pours Himself out for His children. He pours forth His self-sacrificing love that is perfectly demonstrated by this name.

When connected with "El", the definition signifies one who is mighty to nourish, supply, and satisfy. But when applied to God, the meaning is intensified; therefore, it comes to mean one who sheds forth, pours out sustenance and blessing. He is the all-sufficient and all-bountiful.

Read Genesis 49:24–25. In this passage, we see God (El) as the one who helps, but it is the Almighty (El Shaddai) who abundantly blesses with all manner of blessing even from the breast, which refers to the chest or heart of a man.

The Septuagint was translated by Jewish scholars from Hebrew to Greek 250 years before Christ. In it the name "Shaddai" was rendered a number of times by the Greek word *ikanos,* meaning all-sufficient. Thus, it has come to carry this meaning in our current English Bibles.

We are introduced to El Shaddai for the first time in Genesis 17:1–6. In this passage, God allowed the promised son for Abram to wait until it was not humanly possible for his own strength to produce the offspring. It is here that God reveals His sufficiency to revive the deadness of Sarah's womb. This was to teach them that what God promises, only *God* can give!

In Genesis 17, God also makes abundant promises to Abram that only God can fulfill due to their abundance. Read through the chapter and ponder what is so "undoable" about them.

In the midst of this, God asks Abram to walk before Him blamelessly. To walk blamelessly is referring to his walking with God wholeheartedly, with completeness and openness before his God. God alone is the one who can make this happen for Abram or for us. Therefore, we are actually called, as Abram was, to walk closely to our God in order to fulfill this calling of relationship with Him.

El Shaddai then pours His Spirit into us and then through us He blesses others. He demonstrates this through Abram's name change in Genesis 17:5.

> No longer will you be called Abram; your name will be Abraham, for I have made you a father of many nations.

Abram's name meant "exalted father," until El Shaddai stepped in and made it Abraham, which meant "father of many nations." God also added the blessing of fruitfulness to Abraham in verse 6 and the repeated syllable "He" of His own name (YHWH). This represented God's own presence with Abraham. He added this same syllable when He changed Sarai to Sarah as well. One commentary puts it this way,

> El Shaddai gives Himself perfectly to Abram [making him Abraham] and Abraham gives himself perfectly to God. And by God is made fruitful.[24]

We must be like Abraham, willing to surrender our own will in all things and be willing to receive the

Spirit's lead. Though the Spirit of God is freely given to those who place faith in Christ, we will only receive in the measure that we are emptied of all self-will and self-confidence. By this, we are made fruitful for the kingdom. Are you willing to believe and trust Him? Are you willing to let Him do as He wills in your life?

DAY 1

MEMORY VERSE:

> He who dwells in the shelter of the Most High will rest in the shadow of the Almighty.
>
> Psalm 91:1

Begin in prayer this week, asking the one who pours out to open the eyes of your heart and pour out His healing word to minister to your spirit. Take a moment to write the memory verse on a card to carry with you, and remember to practice it often this week.

As we begin a new name of God, let's not forget those names we have previously studied. God is fully all of these names (and so much more) all at once. He never stops being one name to be another. This is similar to us as women.

What are some names you are known by?

_____

_____

It may include anything from your first name, nickname, or Ms. So-and-So to Mommy, friend, honey, dear, sweetheart. I know I have been called many things in my life ... not all good. But I am most blessed to be called "child of God." How about you?

We do not stop being mom to be sister or friend. God (on a much grander and more beautiful scale) does not stop being a God of creation and relationship in order to be a God of judgment or covenant. The God we serve is mighty and perfect in all His ways and all His names.

We learned that the first occurrence of El Shaddai was in the midst of an interaction between Abraham and God. Abraham left that encounter with purpose, faith, and a new name! As we look a bit deeper into this encounter, let's pray for some revelation for our own purpose, increased faith, and a fresh out-breathing of God into our own weary souls.

Read all of Genesis chapter 17.

According to the beginning of the chapter, what does God command Abraham to do?

1. _____

2. _____

God gives Abraham two clear commands. He tells him to walk before Him *and* to be blameless. To be blameless is not equal to being sinless. It literally means to walk wholeheartedly and completely before God. Psalm 26:1 teaches that a blameless life is one of trusting the Lord, and Psalm 19:13 teaches a blameless life is one where we do not have a sin ruling over us and we are not premeditating sin.

Let's look at the other command God gives Abraham. God tells him to "walk before me." The Hebrew word here translated "before" is the word translated *pamea.* It means face, surface of or in front of; meaning to walk facing something.[25] It is the same word used twice in Exodus 33:11.

Fill in the verse below:

> The LORD would speak to Moses _____ to _____, as a man speaks with his _____.

I desire intimacy like that with the Lord. We can have it, too. Moses was not chosen for intimacy because of *Moses,* but because of the relationship-driven *God* that he served. We serve the same God. Praise Him!

The main point of the word *pamea* is all about keeping my face always toward the Lord. That is where intimacy with Him grows. It is the same concept taught in John 15:4–7. What does verse 4 begin with?

_____

Depending on your translation, the English word used is either "remain" or "abide." It is the same concept that the Exodus passage was illustrating. And the same concept God was trying to teach Abraham and us. He so desires to walk intimately with you that He is saying, "Turn your eyes to Me, child. Keep gazing at Me."

When we first fall in love with someone, we can't stop looking at the object of our affection. We study him, think about him, talk about him and talk *to* him as much as possible. God desires that kind of intimacy. He wants us to study Him, think about Him, talk about Him, and talk to Him. Not because He *needs* it, mind you. But because *we* need it!

Let's look at another example of this. Read Psalm 25:14–15. What does the psalmist say is the motive behind keeping his eyes on the Lord?

_____

The enemy of our souls is real, and he is out to trap us! Satan has set snares for you and for me. He tempts us, lures us in and whispers lies to us about God and about ourselves. But when we have our eyes on the Lord, on our El Shaddai, our feet will be released from those snares. God will give us insight and strength to either avoid the snare or He will provide a way out of it (1 Corinthians 10:13).

What does it look like for us to keep our face toward El Shaddai? For Abraham, it included waiting on God's timing for a child and trusting God's plan and God's way. What does it mean for you in your life?

_____

_____

_____

Just as God brought about His plan despite Abraham's weak body and Sarah's "dead womb," El Shaddai is the God who does *not* depend on what we have or don't have, what we can or cannot do, but rather on who He is. And He is enough! God Almighty creates life independent of the laws of His creation. He provides for us by means of His own power.[26]

Lay out your heart before the Lord, acknowledge your own weakness, and ask Him to provide, in the midst of it by His own power.

DAY 2

Begin in prayer today, asking the one who pours out to open the eyes of your heart and pour out His healing word to minister to your spirit. Take a moment to review the memory verse too.

Today let's dig into the main "functions" or purpose God has for revealing Himself as El Shaddai to us. The name means sufficient, super abundant, pourer forth, breasted one.[27]

God desires to be our only sufficiency. He desires to pour out Himself to fill us up in the very places we have need. The thing about God is He does not run low when He pours Himself out. We can continually come and seek more of Him, and there will always be an abundance.

Have you ever felt overwhelmed, defeated, and needy? Do the demands of work, marriage, parenting, family, friendships, service, and life cause you to feel like you are drowning at times? When you run to your El Shaddai, you will never come away empty. He is the supplier, filler, and satisfier of our souls. He ministers right to the deepest need, if we will seek Him for it. It is what we are made for.

Read Psalm 91. This psalm mentions several names of God, so we will look at this psalm closer in a few weeks. For now, remember El Shaddai is translated "Almighty" in this psalm. According to this psalm, what are some of the blessings we can experience when we are in an intimate relationship with the Lord? Nearly every verse of the psalm has one.

What does the psalmist specifically mention about El Shaddai (the Almighty) in verse 1?

The word translated "shadow" here is the original word *sel,* and it means to shade or overshadow; it is used figuratively to indicate protection from adversity or enemies. It is the root word translated "image," in Genesis 1:26. [28]

Read Genesis 1:26, and substitute the word "shadow" for the word "image" as you read the verse. What new insight does this give you?

You and I were made in the shadow of El Shaddai. Go back to Psalm 91:1 now, and read the verse with this in mind.

You and I were made to dwell in the shelter or protection of the presence of Most High (El Elyon, a name we will soon study), and then we can rest in the shadow of El Shaddai.

We spend our lives trying to make a name for ourselves, to be important, to get noticed, accepted, and liked. We pursue money, power, and material things that will never satisfy. We live in the lies that either we are worthy of much praise and applause, or we are unworthy to even lift our head. According to the writer of Ecclesiastes, all of our striving is in vain and worthless. Why? Because we are made in the shadow of the one who mightily pours out blessing, protection, and redemption over us. We *do* have worth as a creation of the Creator and in light of Jesus and what He has done. We needlessly busy our lives and weary ourselves, when if we would just dwell in His presence and live before His face, we would find rest for our souls and a refuge and fortress for ourselves.

What does the last phrase in Psalm 91:2 say?

... in whom I _____.

One hot summer day, as the sun blazed, my youngest son and I were coming out of a store and crossing a busy parking lot. I took his hand and began to make our way toward our vehicle. He said, "Mom, I am going to walk in your shadow, so the sun won't be in my eyes." This gave me profound insight to our own walking in the shadow of El Shaddai. Two thoughts came to me:

First of all, in order to remain in my shadow, my son had to get close to me. If he had walked ten feet behind me and decided to just watch for where I went, not only would he then have the sun beating down on him and blinding him, but he would be completely exposed to the traffic of the busy parking lot. In the same way, our Father desires us to draw near to Him in order to remain in His shadow and receive the rest and peace that comes from that. My son could rest in my shadow as we walked to the car, knowing I would lead the way.

Second, just as my son could not see the cars from around me, so he had to trust me. In the same way, we have got to trust God. *We* can't see the whole picture. If I went right, my son went right without question. He trusted that I knew where the car was and how to get there; that was good enough for him. Our El Shaddai knows where we need to go and how to get there. Do you really believe that? It is only when we get that belief all the way into our hearts that we can begin to trust that God's ways work and begin to walk in them.

As you ponder these thoughts, spend time asking the Lord to show you the condition of your own heart. Are you having trouble taking His hand with the faith of a child? Why? What do you believe will happen if you trust Him fully and begin to walk in His ways? Expose your heart to Him, and ask Him to show you truth that will minister to you right where you are. He loves you so much and has a desire to bring you refuge and rest.

Begin in prayer, asking the one who pours out to open the eyes of your heart and pour out His healing word to minister to your spirit. Remember to take a moment to review the memory verse too.

As we have been getting to know who our El Shaddai is, I pray it is penetrating our hearts. What words come to mind now when you think about "El Shaddai"?

_____

He is by nature one of blessing, pouring out, sustenance, and nourishment. Keep this all in mind as we peer into Isaiah's vision, and try to catch a glimpse of our El Shaddai in all His glory.

Read Isaiah 6:1–8 and visually picture the incredible scene. Remember as you read that "Lord" is Adonai; "Lord Almighty" is El Shaddai (the NASB translates it Lord of Hosts because the literal name used is a derivative of Shaddai, not the literal title "Shaddai," but it gets the same picture across to us); and "Lord" is Yahweh.

Where did Isaiah see God?

_____

Isaiah was getting a glimpse, in the wake of his nation's king's death, of who the real, eternal King is.

There was much activity in Isaiah's vision as well. What were the six wings of the seraphs doing?

_____

_____

_____

This has much significance for us. The creatures that look upon the face of Shaddai cannot help but cover their faces in humility, cover their feet in service to Him, and offer ongoing praise for His holiness. What an example for us, the very ones made in His image and for His glory.[29]

By what name did these creatures call God?

_____

What were the seraphs saying about Shaddai?

_____

_____

_____

We have no idea, nor can we even begin to imagine what goes on in the spiritual realm around us. But these seraphs could clearly see the whole earth is full of Shaddai's outpoured glory. Why then are _we_ missing it?

Glance over at Genesis 1:28. To whom was the command here given?

_____

What did God tell them to do?

_____

_____

The whole earth, according to the seraphs, is filled with the glory of God. If the command was for *man* to fill the whole earth; then it stands to reason that we are the glory of God. We are made to offer Him praise, honor, and worship. This truth offers us significance. We have worth because God made us for His glory to fill the whole earth. Even the seraphs see it! We ought to cry out with the psalmist.

> Praise be to his glorious name forever; may the whole earth be filled with his glory. Amen and amen.
>
> Psalm 72:19

El Shaddai acts with abundance ... superabundance! He fills to the max and beyond. He set stars in the sky, not ten or even a hundred, but billions upon billions. His nature is to pour out generously, especially upon His children. Our problem comes when we fail to see with spiritual eyes, and we look with the limited eyes of man. We think God should pour out money, materially and tangibly, when He says, "I have a far greater provision with much further reaching results than your mind can even fathom." When we catch a glimpse of the reality of who He is, we fall face down in humility to serve the one who fills us to overflowing with Himself for His glory.

What is Isaiah's reaction to this vision in Isaiah 6?

_____

_____

_____

_____

God made atonement for Isaiah and His people, as He has made atonement for us through Jesus Christ. See Romans 3:22–26. This is the "gospel" or "good news."

Therefore, in light of that, what does the Master, Adonai, ask of Isaiah?

_____

_____

_____

_____

What is Isaiah's response?

_____

What does Titus 2:11–14 tell us to do in light of the truth of the gospel? (v. 14)

_____

We are called to "do good," to live as a praise of His glory (Ephesians 1:14), and to share the gospel through the example of our speech, our life, our love, our faith, and our purity (1 Timothy 4:12). Is this how we are living? If not, what changes do you need to make? Are you willing to do it, in light of the truth He has shown you?

He already knows your heart, but when you come unveiled before Him, He will reveal truth and heal your heart with His Word (Psalm 107:20).

DAY 4

· ·

Begin in prayer, asking the one who pours out to open the eyes of your heart and pour out His healing Word to minister to your spirit. Remember to take a moment to review the memory verse too.

Today, we will look into the reflection of El Shaddai in the New Testament, in the form of Jesus Christ. First, let's see El Shaddai illustrate Himself as the one who nourishes and supplies as the bridge from the Old Testament. Begin by reading Exodus 16:11–23.

Describe what happened in this passage. What did the Lord supply? To whom did He supply it? How much of it?

_____

The best way to study God's Word is to let Scripture interpret Scripture. If you read about a person, an occurrence, or a concept in the Word and want to know more about it, often the best place to start is by searching it out in other places in Scripture.

So let's read the commentary provided in Deuteronomy 8:10–18. In this passage Moses is speaking to the Israelites as they prepare to *finally* enter the Promised Land. Moses is summing up the commands for the new land, the Promised Land. He is reminding them to not forget the Lord when all is well in the Promised Land. What a lesson can be learned in that point! But for our lesson, look carefully in verses 16–18. He speaks specifically to the instance we saw in Exodus.

What is he warning them about, regarding the manna?

_____

_____

God alone was their supply. He provided the manna, the quail, and the water from a rock. From His own unquenchable supply, He provided all their needs and even their desires. Psalm 105:40 adds a comment about this. What does it say?

_____

_____

Our El Shaddai desires to fill our souls to satisfaction with Himself!

Let's look more specifically at the manna. It's a beautiful illustration used throughout the ages by the rabbis to represent the Torah (God's Word).

What does Psalm 119:103 say about God's Word?

_____

This is demonstrating the parallel used between the sweet manna and the Word of God. Now let's eavesdrop into a teaching Jesus gave in John 6:30–33. Who is He speaking to? Glance back over the chapter.

_____

According to verses 32–33, who is the supplier?

_____

What does He supply?

_____

Our Supplier and Satisfier, our El Shaddai, is not speaking of supplying a "what" but rather a "who." Jesus is saying to these people that He is the Word made flesh. Now read on to verses 34–37, what does Jesus claim in verse 35?

_____

To these first century Jews, He was clearly drawing a parallel from the manna their forefathers ate in the desert, to the Word of God, and ultimately to Himself. The bread is unique in what it provided. This bread is the bread of life. The word in verse 35 translated "life" is the Greek word *zoe,* meaning the element or principle of life in the spirit and soul; it is used most often in reference to eternal life.[30]

He is saying that this manna would lead to eternal life (*zoe*). But, as is the way of our El Shaddai, He does not stop at our supply. Read John 10:10 and let's see how far He does go.

What contrast was Jesus talking about, and what did He come to give according to John 10:10?

_____

_____

_____

The thief is referring to our enemy, Satan. Now look at the word describing the kind of life Jesus desires to give. Some translations say "abundant", some say "to the full." The original Greek word here is *perissos*, meaning around, over and above, more than enough, exceedingly, superabundantly.[31]

This verse is saying Jesus came to give us an exceedingly, superabundant, spiritual, and eternal life. This has nothing to do with making lots of money or living the "good life." Rather it speaks of living at peace, in continual fellowship with God and denying ourselves as we trust Him. This kind of life is a life that is so filled up with Jesus that it overflows in humble service, compassion, and love for others. That is the kind of life that demonstrates to the world what bread we are feeding on.

Do you see the parallel with the Bread of Life and El Shaddai? Our Supplier feeds His people from His fullness. Now read John 1:14–18. What does John 1:16 say?

_____

_____

If Jesus is our El Shaddai and He pours out from His fullness to fill us up, then why do we walk around empty? What you have studied is truth, so what do you need to do to line your heart up with that truth? Ask the Lord to show it to you.

Is there a verse you need to memorize in order to get truth into your heart and soul (not just head knowledge)? Do you need to make daily time for the Lord, in order to spend time feasting on the Bread of Life each morning? Humbly bring your thoughts before El Shaddai, and ask Him to fill you to overflowing.

DAY 5

Begin in prayer, asking the one who pours out to open the eyes of your heart and pour out His healing word to minister to your spirit. Remember to take a moment to review the memory verse too.

When we met our Heavenly Father as our Creator a couple of weeks ago, we discovered He does not create from afar. He engages His creation in the activity. We know this is true by the very nature of human conception and birth. God has chosen to bring us alongside and allows us to participate in creating a new life. We can see this concept not only demonstrated in Elohim, but we also see it revealed through El Shaddai.

Remember God's encounter with Abraham? He engaged Sarah and Abraham in the creation of Isaac. They conceived him and bore that promised child. El Shaddai did not hand them a fully formed baby, but rather chose to work it out *through* them. Let's see how our Bread of Life reflects this aspect of the name, as well.

Read Matthew 14:13–21. What did the Supplier provide?

_____

According to verse 19, how did He engage His disciples in order to work this miracle through them?

_____

_____

Now glance at the same account in John 6, and see who else He chooses to engage in verse 9. Who was it?

What a God we serve! He could have just chosen to fill their stomachs supernaturally, not having to go through this exchange. The extent of the whole episode could have been solved with a sudden miraculous filling of everyone's stomach ... but no! Our God is a God of relationship. He chooses to engage the people, the boy, and the disciples. They all saw, tasted, and participated in the miracle, and you know they did not soon forget it.

Now look back at Matthew's description (Matthew 14:13–21). How much did the people eat according to verse 20?

El Shaddai, in the cloak of human flesh, poured Himself out until the people were satisfied. Our God desires to satisfy our deepest need *with Himself*. His desire to meet your need exceeds your desire to have your need met.[32] Do you and I really believe that? Do we turn to that when we are weary, anxious, frustrated, or facing temptation?

What desire do you need satisfied? Spend a quiet moment with El Shaddai, and read through the following verses in your time with Him. Ask Him to increase your faith. He is the author and initiator of it.

- Psalm 90:14
- Psalm 103:5
- Psalm 145:16–19

JUST BETWEEN
GOD AND ME

_____

_____

_____

_____

_____

_____

_____

_____

_____

_____

_____

_____

_____

_____

_____

_____

_____

_____

_____

_____

_____

_____

WHO IS YAHWEH RA'AH?

Our God is a storyteller. He enjoys painting illustrations and making parallels to help His people better understand His heart and His desire for us. The most used picture in Scripture to represent the relationship of God to His people is that of a shepherd to his sheep. As our shepherd, He is our Yahweh Ra'ah.

The primary meaning of the Hebrew word *ra'ah* (also spelled "ro'eh" in English) is to feed, lead to pasture, or to shepherd. The word can be used in the relationships between a prince with his people, his priest or a prophet (see Jeremiah 3:15). The word can also be associated with companion or friend as in Exodus 33:11. Therefore it can signify "to associate with, take pleasure in, or cherish something as treasured".[33]

In *The Names of God*, the author paints a beautiful picture of how our Yahweh is our Ra'ah. He says,

> Yahweh is sublime in purity and glorious in majesty, whose thoughts and ways immeasurably transcend the thoughts and ways of His people (Isaiah 55:8–9). Yet the wonderful grace of Yahweh as expressed by the word "shepherd" is such that He can descend to such a relationship with mortal, sinful creatures, whom He has redeemed.[34]

What a beautiful picture of the leadership and love of our Great Shepherd.

The most direct and personal occurrence of Yahweh Ra'ah is found in the twenty-third Psalm. This Psalm gives the illustration of both the activity of the Shepherd and the activity of the sheep.

Let's look a bit into the activity and needs of sheep. And see how you and I could possibly relate to this animal.

> The Palestine shepherd lives day and night with his animals. He establishes a degree of intimacy with them which is touching to observe. He calls them all by their names, and they, knowing his voice and hearing his only, heed. He protects the sheep from thieves and preying animals that would devour them at night, by sleeping in the opening of the often makeshift sheepfold and they, sensing his watchfulness, fear no evil. He provides pasture and water, even in the wilderness and in the presence of enemies and they, casting all their anxiety upon him, are fed. There is a singular communion between the shepherd and his sheep which, after one has visited Palestine and observed it, makes the symbol of the Good Shepherd particularly apt and the 23rd Psalm strangely moving.[35]

Sheep need several things, most importantly, to intimately know their shepherd's voice so they will not go astray. The same is true of us; the more intimately we know Him, the less likely we are to stray from Him. So how do we press in and get to know His voice? It is in the same way as sheep do; we must spend time in our Shepherd's presence in order to better know Him and recognize His voice.

The needs of a sheep, and us, boil down to three main categories:

First of all, sheep need provision. By this, I mean they need nourishment. God provides our nourishment and provisions as promised in Deuteronomy 8:3, 1 Peter 2:2, and Hebrews 5:13–14.

Secondly, sheep need peace. They thrive with calmness and freedom from anxiety. They need freedom from fear, worry, and fighting. Sheep are very competitive and will bite each other when fighting; this can cause the whole herd to get into an uproar. Sound like anyone you know? Maybe more like the sheep in the mirror than we care to admit. How does God provide our peace in the following instances in Scripture, 1 John 4:16–18, Psalm 56:3–4, 1 Peter 5:7?

Finally, sheep need protection. They need to know they are protected from attacks because sheep are prey to many animals. Sheep also need protection in the form of discipline from the shepherd, without it they can harm themselves or each other. God provides us protection in the form of discipline as well, see Proverbs 13:24, Proverbs 29:15. Also read Proverbs 2:8, Psalm 91:14 and notice God's protection over His own sheep.

What about us? How are you and I like sheep in the fold of God, the Good Shepherd? What are your needs right now in this season of your life? How can Yahweh Ra'ah meet you where you are to bring back into the sheepfold, providing your provisions, your peace, and your protection?

DAY 1

MEMORY VERSE:

> The Lord is my shepherd; I shall not be in want. He
> makes me lie down in green pastures, he leads me
> beside quiet waters, he restores my soul. He guides
> me in paths of righteousness for his namesake.
>
> Psalm 23:1–2

Begin in prayer, asking Yahweh Ra'ah to reveal Himself to you through His Word. Spend a moment writing the memory verses on an index card and begin to work on memorizing them.

In our introduction of Yahweh Ra'ah, we discussed some of the needs of sheep. Go over that list; which of these do you relate to in this season of your life?

_____

_____

Of all the needs of sheep, we boiled it down to three categories: They need *provision* (nourishment), *peace* (from worry, fear, and fighting), and *protection* (discipline and free from attacks).

I encourage you to use your Bible's concordance or a source like biblegateway.com to search out some verses of truth pertaining to which one of these you are most struggling with right now. Then begin to work on memorizing those verses or carry them with you and speak their truth into your soul when you begin to hear the same old lies or feel the weakness coming.

Let's see in Scripture why we can apply all these "sheep truths" to ourselves. After reading each passage, write the common denominator:

- Psalm 44:22
- Psalm 100:3
- Isaiah 53:6
- Jeremiah 50:6
- Matthew 9:36

What can you say, but "Baaa?" God does not call us sheep as an insult, but rather to open our eyes to a parallel. The people of antiquity were very familiar with the ways of sheep. Most people in the Middle East, at the time, had sheep. Shepherding was common; it is still not a lost art in that part of the world. As Americans, we have to stretch our minds a bit to see the beauty of this parallel.

We may relate better to the thinking that the sheep and his shepherd were much like loving parents and children. The children's vast needs are best met by loving, caring, and connected parents. The parents supply both love and discipline in the best interest of the child. In a positive parent-child relationship, the child trusts the parent, and the parent's presence supplies comfort for the child. Such it is with sheep and their shepherd. When the sheep get to know the shepherd, they are comforted by his presence and his voice.

As sheep of His pasture, are you growing in relationship with God in such a way that you are easily comforted by His presence and His voice, not just dependent on His activity in your life? If not, what has to happen for you to come to that level of trust?

_____

_____

_____

_____

As you just read in Isaiah 53:6, we, like sheep, have gone astray, each of us to his own way. We often fail to trust God, not because He is not trustworthy, but because we have believed the lies of the enemy and of the world and chosen to go our own way. Close your time today in prayer, asking the Lord to reveal areas where you, the sheep, are failing to trust Him as your Shepherd.

DAY 2

Begin in prayer, asking Yahweh Ra'ah to reveal Himself to you through His Word. Spend a moment practicing your memory verses.

The most beautiful illustration of Yahweh Ra'ah is revealed in the classic psalm, Psalm 23. Over the next two days, we will dig into this psalm and apply its truths to our lives. In it, we will clearly see the role of a good shepherd and the role of sheep defined. Begin by asking the Lord to let this psalm vividly come to life for you, whether it is the first time or the millionth time you have read it. Then read Psalm 23 carefully.

The psalm has a shift right in the middle of the six verses. Do you see it? The first three verses, our memory verses this week, speak *about* the shepherd. The last three verses speak *to* the shepherd. That, in itself, is such a revealing concept. When we are speaking praises to others about our God, it causes us to look to Him, and we can't keep from praising Him directly.

This psalm was written by David, the shepherd made king. As a shepherd himself, David knew well the shepherd's responsibilities and stresses of caring for sheep.

He opens his psalm proclaiming the name Yahweh Ra'ah, literally "YHWH Shepherd." As Yahweh He is the eternal, self-existent God of revelation and the God of His covenant. He is a just and holy God. But as shepherd, He is a caring and nurturing God.

Now, look again at Psalm 23 in your Bible. Take a moment to read verses 1–3 again. According to these verses, what does "He" (the Shepherd) do? List the verbs after the word "He" in each statement.

_____

_____

_____

_____

The sheep need only to follow and trust the shepherd. He is the one taking care of everything. The ancient Judean hillside was a barren dry land, full of thorns and low on grass. In order for a sheep to graze, a shepherd had to come and work the land thoroughly in order to plant seed and produce the tender shoots of grass the sheep liked best. The sheep would not lie down to rest unless they were made comfortable. Sheep are picky. I can sure relate. When was the last time you had much on your mind, yet fell right to sleep comfortably? Not easily accomplished, right? If not impossible! Sheep are the same way, all must be well and comfortable for them to lie down and rest peacefully. In order for that to be the case, much work had to be put forth by the shepherd first.

In verse 2, how is the grass described?

_____

What did the sheep do?

_____

For the sheep to lie down in green pastures, they were essentially lying down in the finished work of their shepherd.

What did Jesus say about His work in John 19:30?

When you and I rest in the salvation we have received through the death, burial, and resurrection of Jesus Christ, we are resting in the finished work of our Shepherd. Are you trusting in His finished work on the cross for your salvation? Or are you attempting to get to heaven through good works, charity donations, or being a nice person (Ephesians 2:8)? We are to examine ourselves to see if we are in the faith (2 Corinthians 13:5). Ask God to search your motives and reveal what you are trusting in.

Sheep are easily frightened and need very clear water since they are also easily susceptible to disease. The freshest water is that which runs through rocks to be filtered, but the rush of water could easily frighten them. Are we not easily frightened by even our own imaginations at times? I don't know about you, but especially when I can't sleep at night, my thoughts can give way to a thousand vain imaginations. Thankfully, our Shepherd leads us beside quiet waters, not waters of fear and terror. Life is hard, and tragedy does happen. But our Good Shepherd gives us the grace we need in the moment we need it. Therefore, we need not ponder the lies our minds conjure up. They lead only to fear and unrest, just like for the sheep.

What does 2 Corinthians 10:3–5 say we ought to do with the thoughts that threaten to set themselves up against the truth of God?

In order to take them captive, we must recognize them. Ask the Lord to reveal them to you and begin to notice when you "chew" on them and begin to replace them with the truth of His Word. The result will be a restored soul, as Psalm 23:3 says.

The original word translated "restored" in the NIV is the word *sub*. It means to turn back, to turn around, return, it essentially denotes movement back to the point of departure.[36]

We can rest in the provision of our Shepherd, trust in His finished work, and take captive our thoughts and make then obedient to truth. Then we return to the place in our relationship with the Lord where we began to pull away from Him and trust in ourselves. When we sin, pull away, and lose fellowship with our Shepherd, we merely need to call out like a wandering sheep, and He will come and return us to the place of fellowship through His Son Jesus (1 John 1:9).

Are you in a place of needing restoration from the Shepherd? Take a moment to acknowledge that in prayer, and listen as He speaks His love over you (Zephaniah 3:17). He will then begin to guide you once more in the path of righteousness—His way and for His namesake!

How has the Good Shepherd spoken to you today?
How is He asking you to respond?

_____

_____

_____

DAY 3

Begin in prayer asking Yahweh Ra'ah to reveal Himself to you through His Word. Spend a moment practicing your memory verses.

Today we will continue our look into Psalm 23. Begin by slowly reading it again; remembering what you learned about the first half of the psalm yesterday. Now we will shift our focus to the second part of this psalm. Do not lose sight of those first few verses, since it forms the backdrop for today's segment.

As we determined earlier, the psalmist opens the psalm speaking *about* the Lord and ends speaking *to* the Lord. Where is the shift? The first part of verse 4 provides the pivot. What does the psalmist say in this part of verse 4?

_____

_____

_____

He goes from praising God to noticing he is in the valley of the shadow of death. We live in a fallen world, greatly affected by death on every level. Everything living around us dies—plants, bugs, animals, and people. We, too, will die. It is part of the curse of sin entering the world. Life is just that, a walk through the valley in the shadow of the inevitable death. Sometimes we may notice it more so than other times.

When someone dies or is diagnosed with a terminal illness, we may see the dark overcast of the shadow. When was the last time you were made keenly aware of the shadow of death?

_____

One day the shadow will dissolve as we step into the truth of 1 Corinthians 15:53–57. Read the passage.

What will death be swallowed up in?

_____

Who gives us that victory according to verse 57?

_____

Knowing the victory over death will be won by the Lord Jesus, we can trust His ways. Where does the psalmist find his comfort, according to the rest of Psalm 23:4?

_____

The presence of his Lord brought him comfort through the valleys. Isaiah, the prophet, was comforted with this same assurance from the Lord. Read Isaiah 43:1–5. It was originally written for the Jews. As New Testament believers, it is a concept we can claim since it is consistent with the whole council of God's Word. Fill in verse 2:

_____ you pass through the waters, _____ _____ _____ _____ _____; and _____ you pass through the rivers, they will not sweep over you. _____ you walk through the fire, you will not be burned; the flames will not set you ablaze.

It does not say the Lord will keep us from going through trials. It says "when" these things happen, because they do happen. Illnesses come, tragedy strikes, pain happens, and people die. But our God is with us. He will see you through and use it for your good. We have such a limited vision of it all. But we can trust the one who sees the whole picture. Just press into Him, He will not leave you.

Psalm 23:4 says He uses His rod and His staff to bring comfort. The rod was an instrument of discipline, and the staff was used to pull the animal out of ditches and to keep them from wandering off. God disciplines and pulls back His own, just as we do.

When children are misbehaving at the park, I call *my* boys and discipline according to their disobedience. I do not call every child at the park to come be reprimanded. They are not my responsibility; *my* sons are! Thus, those who belong to the Lord, He disciplines.

Now let's look at verse 5. This is such a beautiful verse. How is God pictured in the verse? What is His role at the feast where the "table" is?

If God is the servant, then who is being served?

And before whom is this event occurring?

Now that is something to rejoice about! God not only honors and esteems His child, He also serves and blesses His child right in front of their enemies. If you have placed your trust in His salvation, then you are His child. Who are your enemies? Look at Ephesians 6:12.

Our struggle is much greater than an earthly disagreement, no matter how big that seems. The one behind that struggle is not flesh and blood, but Satan and his dark forces. And right in front of him, our Shepherd serves us as guests of honor. He also anoints our head with oil, as kings were anointed. David had seen this in living color, early in his life.

Read 1 Samuel 16:1–13. It describes the prophet Samuel coming, by the Lord's leading, to choose the next king of Israel, God's chosen king. What did Samuel do to signify David's anointing?

Don't miss who was present. The very brothers who aggravated David and figured he would not be worthy of kingship. See 1 Samuel 17:28 for a glimpse into their relationship. Though our war is not with flesh and blood, Satan certainly can use others to bring some aggravation, can't he? Maybe those who thought least of us will one day see the best of us, to the praise and glory of our King.

Glance back to Psalm 23. What is the last phrase of verse 5?

_____

Now let's look at another psalm of David. Read Psalm 16:5–6. In these verses the cup, portion, and lot are synonyms for the word "cup" in Psalm 23. It refers to his position in life. His life is full and even overflowing, according to Psalm 23.

Remember the valley of the shadow of death? Nothing has changed, except the psalmist's perspective. As David has acknowledged the presence of the Lord, he now sees his cup, his lot in life, as overflowing with blessings.

What does it go on to say in verse 6 that follows him?

_____
and _____

He is not saying life will be peaches and cream from here on. He fully understands he is still in the shadow of death, but he sees it through the lens of the truth of God's reality. Our valleys are but for a moment, then eternity!

Read and bask in the truth of 2 Corinthians 4:17–18.

What is seen with our mortal eyes is _____
_____. But what is
unseen is _____. Our eternal glory
_____ outweighs our momentary
troubles. Praise Him!

Spend a few moments in praise to the Lord for
the truths He has spoken over you today. Like David,
we can dwell in the house of the Lord forever. He is
not only our Shepherd, but our Immanuel (God with
us). He is with you. Spend a moment basking in it.

Begin in prayer asking Yahweh Ra'ah to reveal Himself to you through His Word. Spend a moment practicing your memory verses.

Today we will see our Yahweh Ra'ah revealed in the pages of our New Testament. Our God is the same yesterday, today, and tomorrow. He never changes. He loves you the same and desires relationship with you the same as when His precious Son died for you.

Read John 10:11–18. What does Jesus call Himself?

_____

What requirements for a "Good Shepherd" does He give?

_____ (v. 11)

_____ (v. 14)

Now let's see if and how Jesus Himself fulfilled those requirements. The first one is He had to be willing to lay down His life for His sheep. The shepherds of their day did this quite literally. In the evening, they would make a thorn and brush C-shaped enclosure for their sheep. Then through the doorway, they would lead their sheep in, and the shepherd would lie down across the doorway. If any wild animals tried to get in to hurt the sheep, they would have to contend with the shepherd first. This, of course, could put the shepherd's life in jeopardy.

Did Jesus willingly and knowingly lay down His life for His sheep?

(See 1 John 3:16 and John 10:18.) _____ yes _____ no

Now read His reason in verse 13 of John 10. Why does the shepherd do it?

_____

How does that parallel with John 3:16?

_____

Now Jesus does not only lay down His life for His sheep, but what does John 3:17–18 say about what He does?

_____

Jesus gave His life, no doubt about it. Read Luke 24:1–6, but then what did He do?

_____

Without a resurrection, we would not be saved. Many religions have "saviors" or "leaders" they trust in, but those men are dead and buried. They did not have the power to conquer death, as did our Good Shepherd.

The second requirement Jesus gives for the "Good Shepherd" is that they know the sheep and the sheep know Him. The word here translated as "know" is a word that means to have intimate knowledge of another. How are we known according to 1 Corinthians 13:12?

_____

In John 10:15, how does Jesus say He and His sheep should know one another?

_____

The Father and Jesus are one, so it is quite an intimate knowledge of each other. Those who receive Jesus as Savior become one with Him as He comes to reside within us and us in Him. See John 15:5.

Do you know Jesus in a personal and growing relationship?

_____

If so, how can you continue to pursue and grow in that relationship? Jot down some practical ideas, and begin to put them into practice.

_____

_____

Now look at verse 27 of John 10. What does Jesus go on to say is the responsibility of the sheep?

_____

_____

As the sheep, our responsibility is to listen to His voice and to follow Him. Listening requires us to be quiet and still enough to not only take in what He tells us through His Word, but to have the wisdom then to act on it. That is where the "following" comes in. Listening is the easy part. Following Him is the hard part! Though I fail, His grace is sufficient, and He will forgive and set us on the right path once more.

What is the promise of verse 28?

_____

Who or what can remove us from His salvation?

_____ Satan

_____ Our failures

_____ Our sin

_____ Nothing

Take time to soak in the truth of that. Our Jesus is our Shepherd, who lays down His life for His sheep, in order to take it up again and offer it eternally to us. And nothing can pull us out of His sheepfold. Nothing can separate us from His deep love for us (Romans 8:38–39).

DAY 5

Begin in prayer asking Yahweh Ra'ah to reveal Himself to you through His Word. Spend a moment practicing your memory verses.

As we bring this week with our Yahweh Ra'ah to a close, what has been the most significant truth the Lord has revealed to you this week?

_____

_____

   While it is a beautiful truth that our God is our Shepherd, He also assumes a parallel role. Read John 1:29.

How is Jesus introduced by John?

_____

Why?

_____

   Before Christ came and fulfilled the role, unblemished lambs were sacrificed for the sin of the people. But Jesus was the ultimate unblemished lamb. He had no sin and was fully God and fully man. And He was sacrificed for our sins (1 Peter 1:18–19).

This side of glory we cannot wrap our minds around the incredible significance of what the sacrifice Jesus made carries. Let's try to catch a glimpse of it. Read John's revelation of the vision he saw as Jesus revealed the future of mankind to him in Revelation 5:1–4. John is weeping because none is worthy to do what?

_____

If none is worthy, then mankind is lost forever. The scroll represents the redemption of mankind. The opening of the seals is to be done only by one who is worthy before the foundation of the world to open them.

Now read Revelation 5:5–10. How did the elder describe the one worthy (v. 5)?

_____

But according to verse 6, what does John see?

_____

What did His blood do, according to verse 9?

_____

What did it make them? And for what purpose?

_____

_____

_____

Our Yahweh Ra'ah, our Shepherd, is not only the one who nourishes, comforts, and protects. He is the

Lamb who redeems. A good shepherd is necessary, but without redemption, we are headed for eternal hell. Our Lamb is the only one who redeems His people and makes them a kingdom of priests for the purpose of serving our very worthy God. Praise Him!

What has the Lord taught you this week, and how will you respond to Him?

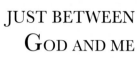

JUST BETWEEN
GOD AND ME

_____

_____

_____

_____

_____

_____

_____

_____

_____

_____

_____

_____

_____

_____

_____

_____

_____

_____

_____

_____

_____

WHO IS YAHWEH SHALOM?

The name of God we will study this week, Yahweh Shalom, calls out to our hearts in a way some of the other names may not. The Hebrew word *Shalom* is a word that means tranquility, wholeness, completeness, restitution, welfare, but above all it means peace. Who couldn't use some of that?

In the Middle East, *Shalom* is a word used for greeting one another. It is called out continually in the streets of those war-torn countries. It reminds me of Jeremiah 8:11 where the prophet quotes the people calling out "peace, peace, where there is no peace." God desires to offer peace to His children, both the Jews and the Gentile believers. But it cannot be experienced apart from His Son, Jesus.

Peace. It is one of the greatest needs and desires of the human heart. It represents the greatest measure of contentment and satisfaction in life. What does true peace look like? I found this example of peace by Ray Stedman in his essay "Need for Peace":

There is a story of artists who were commissioned to paint a picture of peace. One artist depicted peace as an absolutely calm and tranquil sea lying under the moonlight without a ripple on the water. But the one who won the prize pictured a turbulent mountain waterfall, a cataract, with its noisily plunging waters. But half-hidden behind the waterfall, in the midst of all the thunder and tumult, was a bird's nest with a mother bird sitting quietly and serenely on her eggs. That was peace. That is what this offering is all about—peace in the midst of trouble, in the midst of conflict.

In a fallen, sinful world, we can experience true peace in contrast to the turmoil when we turn to Yahweh Shalom.

We can all relate to a lack of peace, tension, restlessness, and a feeling of bondage. No matter what you do, it continues to trouble you and return to your thoughts bringing with it the pressure and negative feelings of unrest.

Our Yahweh Shalom meets us right in that moment, offering the deepest need of our heart as He did for one man in the Scripture's first mention of this name. Read Judges, chapter 6. We see in verse 2 that the unsettled and worried Israelites prepare shelters for *themselves,* rather than seeking out the one who promises to be our Shelter (Psalm 31:20). The Israelites are being severely attacked by their enemy, the Midianites. It is right there, in that turmoil that Yahweh Shalom shows up.

Gideon responds as most of us would, with fear and trepidation. He is the least of the least and has lived with unrest so long, he is not sure he'd recognize peace if it slapped him in the face. Oh, but how wrong he is when peace comes in the form of the one who meets our every need. Yahweh assures Gideon of His presence (v. 12, 16). Now *that* is true peace!

In the midst of his realization of who he was speaking to, Gideon proclaims God as his Adonai, his Lord and Master. This was his way of saying, as Isaiah does centuries later, "Here I am. Send me." But he was overwhelmed with intense fear. So the Lord speaks peace over him, and Gideon is moved to respond by building an altar in verse 24 and proclaiming it, "The LORD is Peace." Gideon goes on to experience some testing in his call and relationship to the Lord. But I doubt he soon forgot this truth about his God.

What about us? How do we respond in the midst of turmoil? Let's seek Him for who He is this week, Yahweh Shalom the LORD is Peace, and take notice of His presence in our life.

MEMORY VERSE:

> You will keep in perfect peace him whose mind is
> steadfast, because he trusts in you.
>
> Isaiah 26:3

Begin by prayerfully asking the God of peace to fill
you, as you seek to know Him more through the
revelation of His name. Remember to practice your
memory verse, and take a moment to write it down
today so you can practice it all week.

In the introduction of Yahweh Shalom, we learned
about how vital peace is to the human psyche. If God
created us to know Him and seek relationship with
Him, then it makes sense that He would reveal Himself as the one who meets one of our greatest human
needs, peace.

Through His Word, God acknowledges our need and
brings it to light for us to be aware of it. What does
Psalm 34:14 tell us to do?

_____

_____

In our turning away from evil and seeking to do
good, will we find peace? We may, but not lasting
peace. This verse says that we must also actively seek
peace and pursue it. You want peace? You have to go

after it with all you have. Biblical peace is not the equivalent of lying in a hammock all day with birds chirping around you. It is a very active word.

What is unusual about God's peace is that it is not defined by our outward circumstances. You can lie in a hammock and have no peace, or you can be in the midst of chaotic children, burning dinner, and phones ringing and experience peace. The situation around you does not define the inner tranquility, when you posses the Shalom (peace) of God.

How does Philippians 4:7 describe the peace of God?

_____

What does this peace do?

_____

The peace of God is very unique in that it can actually put a guard around our hearts and our minds. What does a mind controlled by the Spirit of God look like according to Romans 8:6?

_____

Why does it have to be controlled by the Holy Spirit of God in order to produce life and peace? Read Galatians 5:22–23, and see if you can answer that question.

_____

_____

Peace is a product of a life surrendered to Christ. When we choose to walk the way of the Holy Spirit of God, we will be guarded and filled with a peace we may not be able to understand. Have you ever experienced this? When and what was your thinking?

_____

_____

_____

It is true that living day in and day out walking in perfect peace is difficult. We are assaulted by the world, Satan, and even our own flesh, which loves turmoil and disruption. We cannot create peace within our own souls. We need it, but we cannot create it ourselves. Describe a situation in your life that currently challenges your peace.

_____

_____

Let's close our first day of time with Yahweh Shalom, asking Him for His peace that transcends understanding in the very areas we lack it.

DAY 2

Begin by prayerfully asking the God of peace to fill you with His peace as you seek to know Him more through the revelation of His name. Remember to practice your memory verse as you begin.

You do not have to live long to know peace is hard to come by. So, for believers of the Lord Jesus, the question remains, how do we get the peace our soul craves without trying to control our life's situations?

As the seventeenth-century French monk, Brother Lawrence, learned the peace of God is generally in union with the *presence* of God. This wise, godly monk wrote:

> For me the time of action does not differ from the time of prayer, and in the noise and clatter of my kitchen ... I possess God in as great tranquility as if I were upon my knees at the blessed sacrament.[37]

He knew and could sense in his own life, that when he practiced acknowledging the daily moment-by-moment presence of God, there was peace within him. So how do we live our lives in this presence?

What connection between our actions and our minds do the following examples make?

- James 1:8

- Psalm 139:23–24

  _____

- Luke 10:40–41

  _____

When we are lacking tranquility or wholeness of mind, we will act on it, whether consciously or unconsciously. When was the last time you fretted and were anxious about something and it was later revealed in your actions?

_____

_____

_____

If you are like me, you do not have to ponder long before you realize this connection in your own life. I can fret myself half to death over an issue and then turn and be short tempered with my children, even when they had nothing to do with it. Praise God for forgiveness and the opportunity for healing that this can lead to.

Our healing of heart, when we let the Lord tend to us, can lead to peace. Check out the connection in Jeremiah 33:6 and Luke 8:48. Explain the connection between healing, restoration, and true _shalom_ or peace.

_____

_____

_____

We must let Him search us and tend to us, in order to be brought to a place of true fellowship with the Lord and healing of soul. Are you in need of healing, restoration, or just lacking quiet fellowship with the Lord? Spend this time asking the Lord to search you and expose the areas you need Him most and then seek peace *and* pursue it!

DAY 3

Begin by prayerfully asking the God of peace to fill you with His peace as you seek to know Him more through the revelation of His name. Remember to practice your memory verse as you begin.

Yesterday we started digging into the practical "how" of gaining the *shalom* of God that we so desperately need. Today we will look at another "how" that Scripture highlights for us as we seek peace and pursue it.

Fill in the following verses according to the NIV translation.

- Isaiah 9:6

For to us a child is born, to us a son is given, and the _____ will be on his shoulders. And he will be called Wonderful Counselor, Mighty God, Everlasting Father, _____ of _____.

- Zechariah 9:10

He will proclaim _____ to the nations. His _____ will extend from sea to sea and from the river to the ends of the earth.

- Colossians 3:15

Let the _____ of Christ
_____ in your hearts, since
as members of one body you were called to
_____.

Do you see the connection here? There is peace when God is in authority. He is the Prince or Ruler of Peace. His proclamation of peace is in direct relation to His rule; and when His peace rules our hearts, we have true peace. So why do we fight to relinquish authority? Because where there is authority, there is need for submission, and *that* is certainly a touchy subject!

But what does the Word teach us according to Romans 13:1, Hebrews 13:17, and 1 Peter 2:3?

_____

There are authorities set up on every level—within governments, businesses, schools, churches, and even within our own homes.

Who are women to submit to in our homes? (Ephesians 5:22)

_____

Ultimately our authority is the Lord, in *every area* of submission. When we allow *Him* to rule in our hearts, minds, and soul; then we benefit with a peace that surpasses all understanding.

Being wives who submit to our husbands, or employees that submit to our boss, or citizens that submits to the nation's laws, is not the heart issue. While we ought to submit to these authorities, as we grow in our relationship with Jesus, we see our submission is a heart issue of trusting our Lord with the outcome and control. Do you trust *Him?*

In closing, respond to the Lord, Yahweh Shalom, regarding your need for a submissive heart and a trusting spirit. He is the one ruler who will not let you down.

DAY 4

Begin by prayerfully asking the God of peace to fill you with His peace as you seek to know Him more through the revelation of His name. Remember to practice your memory verse as you begin.

As we have seen our Yahweh Shalom through the pages of Scripture, we cannot help but see Jesus right alongside. It is evident from the first revelation of Yahweh Shalom that Jesus is there. Isaiah's announcement of His coming birth (hundreds of years prior) proclaimed Him as the Prince of Peace.

What does the book of Ephesians tell us about Jesus in chapter 2 verse 14?

_____

Is it any wonder why He would have His fingerprints throughout Scripture as the Prince of Peace? The Greek title "Prince of Peace" is the original words *Sar Shalom*.[38] Do you see the connecting title to the Hebrew name Yahweh Shalom? Do you recall the meaning of "Shalom"?

_____

The title Sar Shalom does not actually appear in the New Testament, but the concept is evident. Listen as the angels proclaim this truth on the night of His birth in reading Luke 2:14.

The Greek word in this verse translated "peace" is the word *eirene* and like its Hebrew counterpart, it is much more than the absence of conflict.

When we experience this peace with God through Jesus, (who is our peace) then we can walk in peace with others.

We will look more at our peace with God tomorrow, but for now soak in Hebrews 13:20–21. Don't miss the reference to the Shepherd here. What does the God of Peace do through the blood of Jesus, beyond reconciling us? (Especially v. 21)

_____

_____

As we mentioned when we discussed creation, God does nothing in vain. He has a plan and purpose for why He created, why He redeems, and why He equips us. His heart's desire is for us to know Him and make Him known in the world. We must be prepared for such a monumental calling. So according to 1 Thessalonians 5:23–24, who does the preparing? And what preparing needs to be done?

_____

_____

_____

Each time I read that passage, I wonder if God is called the God of Peace here to remind us of that truth through the crucial process of sanctification. In order to grow us and purify our faith, God must refine us and strengthen us in godliness. This process can be painful, tiring, and wearisome. Therefore in the midst of it, we are to remind ourselves that He is the goal because He is the God of Peace.

DAY 5

Begin by prayerfully asking the God of peace to fill you with His peace as you seek to know Him more through the revelation of His name. Remember to practice your memory verse as you begin.

As we bring our week of meeting Yahweh Shalom to a close, let's recall our last thoughts from Day 4. The process of sanctification is painful, yet according to 1 Thessalonians 5:23–24, the God of Peace is faithful to do it. It seems contradictory that it often takes effort to obtain peacefulness. It brings to mind a similar contradiction regarding the peace that the Lord Jesus spoke of in Matthew 10:34.

Fill in the verse below:

> Do not suppose that I have come to bring _____ to the earth. I did not come to bring _____, but a _____.

But I thought He was the Prince of Peace, our *Sar Shalom!* As one author agrees, God uses apparent contradictions in His Word to force us to dig.[39] Let's begin by reading Matthew 10:32–42.

According to this passage, whom did Jesus come to divide?

_____

What would He use to divide, according to this Matthew passage?

_____

Well, let's allow Scripture to interpret Scripture. Read Ephesians 6:17, what is the "sword"?

_____

The Word of God certainly brings division. It divides the lost from the saved, the righteous from the unrighteous, the humble from the proud, and the true sheep from the goats. According to Hebrews 4:12, what else does it divide?

_____

His sword certainly came to bring division, but He is our peace, according to Ephesians 2:14.

How did this come about then? Read Colossians 1:15–23.

Why should Christ have supremacy in all things?

_____

What two things pleased God, according to verses 19–20?

1. _____

2. _____

So how did God make the peace?

_____

So what changed and brought us from division to reconciliation? It was the blood of Jesus through His death on the cross!

We could not experience peace with God until the fullness of the Godhead made peace with death.[40]

What does having peace with God mean for us then? Read Ephesians 2:13–18. Fill in verse 18:

For through _____
we both have _____. to
the _____ by one Spirit.

Because of the peace of Christ through the blood of Christ, we have access to the Father. Those who were once far off are now made near to the Father.

What does this truth mean to you personally in this season of your walk with Him? Offer Him praise and thanksgiving.

JUST BETWEEN
GOD AND ME

_____

_____

_____

_____

_____

_____

_____

_____

_____

_____

_____

_____

_____

_____

_____

_____

_____

_____

_____

_____

_____

WHO IS YAHWEH SHAMMAH?

Have you ever felt completely alone? As if no one, not even the Lord was with you? Our head may know His omnipresence to be so, but I pray this week, we learn it in our hearts.

The meaning of the name Yahweh Shammah is "Yahweh is There." In *Names of God* Nathan Stone points out,

> In light of its setting and significance it is a most fitting name with which to climax the Old Testament revelation of God.[41]

Beginning at Genesis with man's original sin, God has desired to ultimately dwell with His children. It was the purpose of the tent and the tabernacles (Exodus 29:42). God's heart is to be *there*, with His people in their midst and dwelling among them (Leviticus 26:11–12).

This name of God is actually the name given to a city rather than to God, but it so closely associated with God's presence and power that it has often been equated with a name of God. Yahweh Shammah reminds us we were created both to enjoy and manifest God's presence.

As I said, this name was first given to a holy city. Read Ezekiel 10:18–19 and 11:22–25, and notice what happened to God's glory. The Lord's glory was His manifest visible presence to the Israelite people. His presence was removed as a result of the people's sin. They had repeatedly turned away from the Lord and toward their own false gods.

Just as we often separate ourselves from our disobedient children, God removed Himself from His own disobedient children. The chastisement was the loss of His presence with His children in Jerusalem. But His heart was still tugged toward His children. So as Ezekiel closes, God gives him prophecy of His own permanent dwelling with His children in Ezekiel 48:35,

> And the name of that city from that time on will be: THE LORD IS THERE.

The naming and proclaiming of this title brought hope to a place that severely lacked hope. Our world still lacks hope. Those who are in Christ with the Holy Spirit of God dwelling within us, carry around the very presence of our Holy God within us. Thus we hold the very hope this world desperately needs.

Yet we live as if there is no hope when we fail to live out Philippians 3:20.

> Our citizenship is in heaven. And we eagerly await a Savior from there, the Lord Jesus Christ.

When we gorge ourselves on the things of this world, we lose sight of heaven's realities (Colossians 3:1–2). We must fix our eyes on those things above, being reminded of the perfect hope we carry and offering it to the lost world around us.

We can refocus our thoughts even this week, as we practice the moment by moment presence of our Lord with us and meditate on truths of His word that offer hope for our future:

- Philippians 3:7–8

- 1 Thessalonians 1:9–10

- 2 Timothy 2:3–4

DAY 1

MEMORY VERSE

> Be strong and courageous. Do not be afraid or ter-
> rified because of them, for the LORD your God goes
> with you; he will never leave you nor forsake you.
>
> Deuteronomy 31:6

Begin your time in prayer to your very present God,
asking Him to reveal Himself to you through His
Word. Take a moment now to write the memory verse
on a card to carry with you this week too. Remember
to practice it often.

One of the most incredible names that our self-
existing, holy, majestic and powerful God chooses
to reveal Himself as is a "there" God. He is a "with
us" God. Yahweh Shammah spoke hope and life and
redemption where there was none. It is so reminis-
cent of our own salvation experiences, isn't it? Do you
remember the day that you, in your hopeless state of
sin, heard the call of a holy God willing to engage in
relationship with you through His Son Jesus? Describe
that realization.

_____

_____

_____

If God's presence gives anything, it's hope. Without His hope what does Psalm 42:5 say is our mental state?

Most of us don't need the psalm to tell us that without God, we are downcast. I lived with depression of soul for years before I turned to Christ. Without Him, I would surely have self- destructed. Can you relate?

Consider this quote:

> The name Jehovah (or Yahweh) sets God forth in His moral and spiritual attributes, the special relationship between Him and the crowning work of Creation, the man made in His image, was a moral and spiritual one. That moral and spiritual relationship was broken by man's disobedience, sin and the fall. After that, the names of God compounded with Jehovah reveal Him as providing redemption for fallen, sinful man, and depicting every aspect of that great transaction of redemption by which man is fully restored to God-healing, victory, peace, sanctification, justification, preservation, care, and guidance. Jehovah-Shammah is the promise and pledge of the completion of that purpose in man's final rest and glory, for man's end is to glorify God and enjoy Him forever.[42]

Did you catch that? The names compounded with Yahweh or Jehovah, (the German translation of Yahweh), reveals God as providing our redemption and full restoration. So if He is Yahweh Shammah, He is the "with us" Redeemer, redeeming lost man for relationship with Him. Amazing, isn't it? So why do we go through life defeated and downcast?

Let's see what truth lies in Psalm 62:5. Fill it in according to the NIV:

Find _____, O my soul, in _____ alone; my _____ comes from him.

When we teach our hearts what our head knows, that God is our hope, then we find rest that allows us to trust Him. Then we can serve others with joy, submit to our husbands with delight, and trust God's heart for our wayward children.

What do you need to know you can trust Yahweh Shammah for?

_____

Do you know He is there, right in the midst of the pain, of the unfairness, of the loss, He is there? Soak in the truth of Psalm 139:1–12. Where can we go to get away from Him?

_____

Even in our darkness, we are not hidden from His light. We only need to look up. He is there and always reaching out for us.

The book of Ezekiel is filled with the pain God's heart feels when we chose to pull away from Him. We cannot "leave" Him, but we can certainly grieve His spirit with our sin and cause His presence and His voice to not be obvious in our life. What does God offer His children through His prophet, Ezekiel, in the vision of dry bones? What revives those dry places? Read Ezekiel 37:1–6.

In verse 4, He tells those dry bones to hear the Word of the Lord and life will come into them. Do you know His Word? Circle on the scale where you feel you are in reference to really knowing God's Word:

1   2   3   4   5   6   7   8   9   10

Scholars spend their lives trying to understand the Word of God, but it is such a deep, rich gem that we will never get to know it all, not this side of heaven. But we can press on to know Him more every day through His Word. And we will reap the benefits of dry bones coming to life as we begin to feel the manifest presence of God in our lives.

What does 2 Timothy 3:16 say about God's Word?

When my son tries to see his breath on the window, he has to stand right up against it and breathe out. I am usually fine until he starts to write on it with his finger. Anyway, the point is, for God to exhale this Word on the page, He is right there every morning exhaling a word for you. If you and I will press ourselves against it through Bible reading, memorization, and prayer, we will be near enough to almost feel the warm breath of God on our faces. Oh, how I want that. How my depraved and weary soul needs it!

Spend time in prayer asking the Lord to reveal His presence to you and give you a hunger for more.

DAY 2

Begin your time in prayer to your very present God, asking Him to reveal Himself to you through His Word. Take a moment to practice your memory verse.

As we press in to know our Yahweh Shammah, let's look at some of the Old Testament revelations He gave of Himself and see how they might apply to us. What does Roman 15:4 say about it?

_____

_____

We determined yesterday, we definitely need some hope. So let's get some Old Testament examples into our hearts.

Begin by reading Genesis 3:8. What does it imply about how God may have revealed Himself before the fall?

_____

_____

Can you imagine walking with God in the garden? Oh, I cannot wait to see Him face-to-face!

Read Exodus 33:20. Why are we hindered from it now?

_____

It would kill us because of our sin and His holiness. We have no idea the vastness and greatness of His holiness and the depth of depravity of our sin. Reading through the book of Ezekiel or Jeremiah, sure helps get some perspective. If you are not familiar with any of the prophet books, you should spend some time reading through them. Though the imagery can be hard to grasp, they are mostly books about the depth of man's sin and the holy heart of God who pursues His children, begging them to turn to Him. He has such a heart for us to know Him.

Now let's see how He revealed Himself to His children after the fall. Read Exodus 13:20–21 and join the Israelites in the desert.

How does God reveal His presence?

_____

What is the "purpose" of His presence here?

_____

Do you need guidance or direction in this season of your life? Where do we go for that?

Too often we seek anything from self-help books to well-meaning friends, when God's heart desires us to first go to Him. His presence can give you direction and guidance. He first and foremost desires relationship with you. As we seek Him for direction, we grow in our walk with Him and more clearly see the way to walk.

While the Israelites were in the wilderness with Moses, God had them build a movable tabernacle called the Tent of Meeting. This was the place where they would make their daily sacrifices to the Lord in order to be made right before Him each day.

Read Exodus 29:10–14. Where was the sin offering sacrifice to be made, according to v. 11?

_____

Now, with that in mind, read Hebrews 10:8–22. Take in every word of truth.

What is our sacrifice through which we have been made holy (v. 10)?

_____

Where are His laws now to be written (v. 16)?

_____

According to verses 17–18, those who trust in the blood sacrifice of Jesus are what?

_____

Therefore we can have _____
(v. 19) to enter the Most Holy Place (the presence of God).

As a result we ought to (verse 22) …

_____

_____

_____

Because He who _____ is
_____. (v. 23)

So, as New Testament believers, is our God still Yahweh Shammah?

_____ Yes _____ No

His presence should be everything to us. Oh, that our hearts would line up with what Moses spoke in Exodus 33. Glance back to Exodus and read chapter 33:12–16, in order to gain context of what is happening. What did Moses beg God for?

_____

Why, according to v. 16?

_____

Isn't that incredible? The presence of God would distinguish them from the other people on the face of the earth. We Christians are an unusual crowd, as we should be. We serve an unusual God, the holy and unique God.

If someone looked at your life, in the recent days and weeks, would they say it is characterized by the very presence of God? Are you distinguishable from all other people on the face of the earth? Ponder this before the Lord as you close today.

DAY 3

Begin your time in prayer to your very present God, asking him to reveal Himself to you through His Word. Take a moment to practice your memory verse.

We have seen God's revelation of His presence in a couple of instances in Scripture. Are you beginning to see His hand in your own personal life? If so, describe a recent example. If not, ask Him to give you eyes to see it, because He is there.

_____

_____

Today, let's walk alongside a couple of biblical characters that uniquely displayed the presence of God at work in their lives. Yesterday we peeked in at Moses and his conversation with Yahweh Shammah.

We could find many examples of King David's walk with his God. Let's look at one and see what "benefit" David was blessed with as a result. Read 1 Samuel 29:11–2. Where had David and his men gone?

_____

What had their enemies done while they were off fighting Philistines?

_____

Read on to David's response in 1 Samuel 30:3–5. Of course they wept. They cried until their strength was gone. Have you ever been so broken you cried out until there was no strength left? Be encouraged; our God can meet you right there. Read verse 6 and fill in the end of it.

But David found _____ in the _____ his _____.

That was a man who knew the presence of a very real God. In the midst of immense pain and loss, he found his strength in the Lord his God!

Now let's look at a few young men who also experienced the very real presence of God. Read Daniel 3:12–18. These men were captured and taken to Babylon to serve the king. They refused to bow to the king of Babylon and worship him. How was the king going to handle this disrespect?

_____

What were Shadrach, Meshach, and Abednego's feelings about it (v. 17)?

_____

_____

So what happened? Read verses 19–27.

_____

_____

_____

Many scholars agree that the fourth man, who "looks like the son of the gods" was Christ Jesus Himself walking around in that fire with the men. The presence of God made flesh. What evidence of God's presence did the three men manifest when they were pulled back out of the fire?

_____

_____

We may never be cast into a fire, we may not be saved from one as literally as they were, but we see the example this illustrates for us. What does this say to you about the presence of God and the result of it?

_____

_____

What does 2 Corinthians 4:7–9 say about us?

_____

_____

Spiritually speaking, those who are in Christ are surrounded by the presence of God and will prevail, regardless of the difficulties and trials we face this side of heaven. We often fail to see things through Christ's eyes, and we limit our vision to earthly shadows—forgetting the reality is far surpassing the mere shadows cast on this planet.

Are there trials that are nearly drowning you right now? Could you use a dose of His presence in the midst of it? Spend time telling Him and seeking Him in the midst of your fire, you just might see a fourth man like the Son of the Living God.

DAY 4

Begin your time in prayer to your very present God, asking Him to reveal Himself to you through His Word. Take a moment to practice your memory verse.

This week we have looked at a few biblical lives touched by the presence of God. Today let's catch a glimpse of His presence right where He intends it to be! Interested? Let's begin in Exodus.

God had given very specific directions for Moses and the skilled men to build a holy tabernacle for the dwelling of His presence. He gave detailed directions for every single object and piece of material in the tabernacle. Now in chapter 40, God gives specific directions for where everything goes. Why is God so specific? Flip over to Hebrews 8:5 then fill in below:

> They serve at a sanctuary that is a _____ and _____ of what is in _____ _____.

God told Moses to make the earthly sanctuary for His glory after a heavenly pattern only He could see. Once Moses and the priests built the earthly replica, a heavenly reality was seen on the dirt of earth.

Now go back to Exodus, and let's notice how God displayed His pleasure for this tabernacle. Read Exodus 40:34–38. What did God's glory do?

Can you even imagine that? What do you think it looked like?

_____

_____

_____

_____

God's glory so filled the temple that Moses could not even enter it! What was God's purpose and desire for the tabernacle? See Exodus 25:8.

_____

God is always after relationship. We, because of sin, cannot reach Him. So in His mercy, He came to us and had Moses build a place for His holiness so He could dwell among His people.

The Hebrew word translated "tabernacle" is *miskan,* meaning a dwelling place, place of residence or habitation. It is also from a root word meaning abiding presence of and the glory of. Therefore, where the abiding presence of the Lord is, where He makes His dwelling, there His glory will be as well.

According to Ezekiel 37:27, where does Yahweh Shammah desire to make His dwelling?

_____

This verse is prophetic and spoken in future tense. This is incredible since the Old Testament tabernacle had been built and used centuries earlier. God was dwelling with His people, right? He had also met with them, at this point, through the stationary temple in Jerusalem that Solomon had built. But what is interesting is God uses the same word translated "tabernacle" in Exodus right here in Ezekiel 37. He literally says, "My tabernacle will be with them."

The Greek translation for this same word is *skenoo* from the root *skene,* meaning tabernacle, live, dwell.[43] Now check out where it is used in John 1:14. Who is this verse referring to?

_____

God tabernacled among His people through His Son, Jesus Christ. And through that tabernacle, like the ones previously, He revealed to us His glory, the glory of the One and Only. But He did not stop there. Read 1 Corinthians 3:16–17. What does this passage call your physical body?

_____

Individual believers are tabernacles of His glory. How do we demonstrate that glory to a lost and dying world? Fill in John 15:8.

This is to my Father's _____,
that you _____ _____,
showing yourselves to be my disciples.

How do you and I bear fruit and what does that look like in the life of a tabernacle filled with His glory? Read Galatians 5:22–23, and ask the Lord to show you what areas of your life need this fruit applied. Then jot down verses that help you live out this fruit and shine the glory of your Father from His earthly tabernacle.

_____

_____

_____

_____

Begin your time in prayer to your very present God, asking him to reveal Himself to you through His Word. Take a moment to practice your memory verse.

Yesterday we began to see how Jesus Christ fulfilled the name Yahweh Shammah, the Lord is There. Today let's look further into this truth. Read Matthew 1:22–23. What does the name given to Jesus in this verse mean?

_____

In an even more incredible act of mercy, God came to meet with fallen man as the "with us" God. He made Himself susceptible to sorrow, pain, and temptation in order to truly abide with His own. In Jesus we see how extreme God's love is.

During Immanuel's earthly ministry, He spoke the words of John 15:1–5. Read these words, and let's see how they apply to us.

Fill in the second sentence of verse 5.

If a man _____ in

_____,

and _____

_____ in _____,

_____ will bear

_____ _____;

apart from _____ you can do

_____.

The word here translated "remain" or "abide" is the Greek word *meno*, meaning to remain, abide or dwell; also to be or remain united with him in heart, mind, and will.[44] When we remain in Christ and He remains in us through His word; then we essentially line up our hearts, minds, and wills with our "with us" God and begin to bear much fruit to the Father's glory.

About what do you need Christ's heart?

_____

About what do you need Christ's mind?

_____

About what do you need Christ's will?

_____

How do we get a Christ attitude then? Read Philippians 2:5–8.

_____

_____

We look most like Christ when we humble ourselves and serve in His name and for His glory alone. When the temple was built, God's people desired to be near it, not because of the building itself, but the one who met with them there. When Jesus came, the disciples could not get enough of Him. The crowds followed Him, not because of the man, but because of who He was. When we love our families, press on in difficult marriages, and reach out to a lost world expecting nothing in return, others see and are attracted ... not to us, but to the one for whom we are ambassadors (2 Corinthians 5:20).

Matthew opened his scroll with a "with us" God, and he closed it with a "with us" God. Read Matthew 28:19–20. What does Jesus command?

_____

_____

What does He promise?

_____

How does that affect you to know your God is very much with you? He came to be with you and left His Spirit so you could remain in Him and He could remain in you. Journal your thoughts as you ponder the incredible truths the Lord has taught us this week.

JUST BETWEEN
GOD AND ME

_____
_____
_____
_____
_____
_____
_____
_____
_____
_____
_____
_____
_____
_____
_____
_____
_____
_____
_____
_____

WHO IS YAHWEH NISSI?

Whether we are following the Lord Jesus or not, every moment there is a spiritual battle going on in the heavenlies around us that we are spared from seeing. Those who are walking with the Lord are His warriors in this battle. Our enemy, the devil, is constantly attacking us. As warriors, we must be prepared and know our Commander well. This week's name of God is one that clearly represents this spiritual battle. It illustrates for us the value of our soul and how God views *us* as one worth fighting for.

Yahweh Nissi means the LORD my Banner. The Hebrew word for "banner" is *nes,* and it literally translates as pole, standard, or symbol; it represents the Lord, and it was used as a place for an army to rally during a battle. The root Hebrew word here is *nasas* and it carried the connotation of sparkling, gleaming, shining, or display.[45] This is such an appropriate illustration when we consider Philippians 2:15, which challenges believers to be blameless and pure, children of God without fault in a crooked and depraved generation in which we are to *shine like stars* in the universe.

Yasa is a related Hebrew word, which means victory, rescue, deliver; it is a word that speaks of the physical deliverance from enemies gained through theological meaning.[46] This word is used in Isaiah 45:22 and is the root word used in Yeshua, the Hebrew translation for Jesus. This makes perfect sense when we consider that our victory over our own enemy, Satan, is won only through Jesus, the living Word of God.

Yahweh Nissi is first introduced in Exodus 17:8–16. In this passage the Israelites, the people of God, are at war against the Amalekites. Now this particular group of people is significant in that they are descendants of Esau (Genesis 36:12). Esau was the brother of Jacob who sold his birthright (eternal implications) for a bowl of soup (temporal implications), thus he fed his own flesh rather than dying to his flesh to feed his soul. The connection with Esau is valuable in providing insight into this war between the Amalekites and the Israelites. Commentaries compare this war to the war of our own flesh. We struggle daily with dying to the temporal desires of our flesh in order to feed eternal desires and grow in our walk with the Lord.

Look back over Exodus 17:8–16 and notice how the victory over this enemy is won. Study verses 12–13 in particular.

> When Moses' hands grew tired, they took a stone and put it under him and he sat on it. Aaron and Hur held up his hands—one on one side and one on the other—so that his hands remained steady till sunset. So Joshua overcame the Amalekite army with the sword.
>
> Exodus 17:12–13

Just as our victory over the flesh can only be won by our focus and praise of the Lord, this earthly battle was won by Hur and Aaron upholding the arms of Moses throughout the duration.

This illustration sets the stage for Yahweh Nissi's introduction in Scripture. When the battle is won, they have no doubt who won that battle. Moses builds an altar and calls it the LORD is my Banner, Yahweh Nissi.

This is a name proclaimed over an altar, rather than directly to the Lord; but just as Yahweh Shammah was so closely associated with the holy Jerusalem, so our Yahweh Nissi is closely associated with the victory over our flesh.

The name Yahweh Nissi is not mentioned in Psalm 20, yet His fingerprint is clearly represented as one who battles for His children. Read Psalm 20 and notice all the activity Yahweh Nissi performs on behalf of His child. I found the repetition of the Hebrew word *male* in verses 4 and 5 very interesting.

> May he give you the desire of your heart and make all your plans succeed. We will shout for joy when you are victorious and will lift up our banners in the name of our God. May the LORD grant all your requests.

The word is translated "succeed" in verse 4 and "grant" in verse 5. But it is the same Hebrew word, which means to fill or accomplish; it is a word that generally denotes the completion of something that was unfinished or the filling of something that was empty.[47]

Our Yahweh Nissi not only stands over us to strengthen us for the battle against sin; He is the one who fills us in the very places we are empty. How effective is a soldier who is empty of weapons, gear, or protection? Such is the same for us, we are called to a battle that requires us to be filled up with the truth of God in our very inward places, in order to be geared up and fight the enemy of our soul.

What area of your life are you needing a victory over sin? We often act out in sin from a wounding we have experienced. Our wounds leave empty, broken places within us. But our Yahweh Nissi comes and meets us in those empty places with the promise of filling them with Himself, His healing, His forgiveness, and His love (Romans 5:5). Then we can gear up for battle with our hands held up in worship to the one who claims the victory for us.

DAY 1

MEMORY VERSE:

> But thanks be to God! He gives us the victory
> through our Lord Jesus Christ.
>
> 1 Corinthians 15:57

Begin by prayerfully asking the Yahweh Nissi to reveal
Himself to you through His Word. Take a moment
to write down the memory verse for this week on an
index card and begin practicing it.

We have learned about our three spiritual enemies.
Can you name them?

_____

God, as revealed in Yahweh Nissi, is the banner
over us in the victory over these enemies. David, the
psalmist, knew God's victory well. He depended on it
both physically and spiritually. Read Psalm 108, and
peek into his relationship with his victorious God.

Who does the Lord save, according to verse 6?

_____

Fill in the following, according to verses 12–13:

> Give us aid against the _____, for
> the help of _____ is
> _____.
> With _____ we will gain the
> _____ he will trample down the enemies.

According to this psalm, the help of man is *worthless*. The original Hebrew word here means false, worthless, that which is vain, denotes anything which is unsubstantial or unreal.[48]

Then why do you think we are so quick to run to man for help or council?

It can certainly require discipline to practice going to the Lord first with our issues, trials, and needs before we go to man (or woman) for help. Calling a friend, sister, mother, or neighbor gives us immediate gratification. After talking to a friend for an hour, have you found that often what could have been a matter of prayer is not so pressing? I have certainly missed opportunities to take things to the Lord because I first took it to a friend.

Not that we lose the chance to take it to Him, He is always there waiting for us to come. But it can certainly keep us from praying if we have already "talked it to death" with someone else.

Though there is help to be found in godly council from a friend who loves Jesus, we ought to first take it to Jesus. Consider the words of this classic hymn:

> What a Friend we have in Jesus,
> All our sins and grieves to bear!
> What a privilege to carry
> Everything to God in prayer!
> O what peace we often forfeit,
> O what needless pain we bear,
> All because we do not carry

Everything to God in prayer!
Have we trials and temptations?
Is there trouble anywhere?
We should never be discouraged,
Take it to the Lord in prayer.
Can we find a friend so faithful
Who will all our sorrows share?
Jesus knows our every weakness,
Take it to the Lord in prayer.
Are we weak and heavy-laden,
encumbered with a load of care?
Precious Savior, still our refuge.
Take it to the Lord in prayer;
Do thy friends despise, forsake thee?
Take it to the Lord in prayer;
In His arms He'll take and shield thee,
Thou wilt find a solace there.[49]

For us to gain the victory over our enemies (world, flesh, Satan) we must take it to Jesus in prayer. Read the following verses, and take note of who gains the victory and from whom it came.

- Joshua 10:7–10

_____

_____

_____

- 2 Samuel 8:5–6

_____

_____

_____

- 2 Samuel 8:14

  _____

  _____

  _____

- Judges 12:3

  _____

  _____

  _____

Our victory comes from whom?

_____

So who shall we carry our burdens to?

_____

Release your burdens to Jesus in prayer and ask Him to remind you to come to Him first.

DAY 2

Begin by prayerfully asking the Yahweh Nissi to reveal Himself to you through His Word. Then remember to practice saying your memory verse.

In our first lesson, we saw the pain we carry when we fail to go to God before going to others. But there is someone else we tend to go to and trust in before casting our cares on the Lord.

Read Psalm 44:1–8 and write down what we tend to trust in other than God, according to verses 6–7.

_____

The reference to a bow and a sword is a reference to our own strength. We often trust ourselves before we trust God for the victory over our sin.

What are some examples that come to mind of what we try to do in our own strength versus going to God?

_____

_____

_____

Don't miss where the psalmist heard this truth of not trusting in his bow or his sword. Glance at verses 1–3. Where did he get this teaching from?

_____

In biblical times, fathers taught their sons the Scriptures. The children were told of all of God's deeds and the children were expected to even memorize large portions of Scripture from a young age. Is this how we are raising our children and grandchildren? Whether we are in a season of parenting or not, we are mentoring our neighbors, our coworkers, and our family in the ways of the Lord, by living our life for Jesus before them. But we must be intentional.

What is the first phrase of Psalm 44:1?

We _____ with our

_____.

This implies that the truths of God were spoken aloud to these men while they were young and impressionable.

Consider the value God places on this generational teaching through the following verses:

- Deuteronomy 32:7

_____

- Deuteronomy 4:9

_____

- Psalm 34:11

_____

Do you have children or new believers in your life right now that need to hear of the good God has done in your life?

_____

If you cannot think of any children or new believers in your sphere of influence right now, ask the Lord to open your eyes to those He has placed around you that need to hear the good news of Jesus. They are there; we just need to notice it.

As you pray to the Lord today, consider those children or new believers He has brought to mind and spend time praying for them. Consider how you will practically and intentionally teach them the testimony the Lord has given you, what He has done and is doing in your life.

DAY 3

Begin by prayerfully asking the Yahweh Nissi to reveal Himself to you through His Word. Then remember to practice saying your memory verse.

The banners of the Old Testament were used to identify the armies with their country. The color and design of the banner would tell which side you were on, what army, tribe, or family you were part of. Read Numbers 2:2 and 1 John 3:1, and write down whose family you are a part of according to 1 John.

_____

What is the banner of God's family? Read Song of Solomon 2:4b and fill it in below:

... His _____ over me is

_____.

The word in this verse translated "love" is an interesting word. It is from the Hebrew word *ahab*, meaning love, desire, delight, like, be fond of, beloved, and a passionate lover. The word implies an ardent and vehement inclination of the mind and a tenderness of affection at the same time.[50] That means that this kind of love is passionate, glowing, and burning. It is a violent love with intense and strong passion. The word also denotes a strong emotional attachment for a desire to possess or be in the presence of the object of love.

Do you realize what that is saying? The Creator God, the Holy One, who placed the stars in orbit and holds all things together by His very word, holds a banner over you in the heavenlies. He displays a passionate, violent, burning love for you that is tender and delightful, which causes Him to desire to be constantly in your presence. What is your response to such love?

_____

_____

_____

_____

Have you ever known such love? Have you ever known it in a healthy way? Often we may feel strongly and passionately about another person but with our corrupt hearts and needy souls, we actually display a codependency and unhealthy attachment to another person. Our hearts were meant to find this kind of passion in Christ. The closest healthy relationship like this I can think of is parenting, specifically motherhood. I love my children so deeply I would die for them. But even this analogy falls short of the pure love of the Father.

What does Matthew 7:9–11 say about our parental love compared to His parental love?

_____

He loves us intimately and passionately like a lover, but with the purity of a mother. His love is tender and intense at the same time. Can you even fathom it?

What do the following verses teach about His love for you?

- Psalm 52:8

_____

_____

- Psalm 61:7

_____

_____

- Psalm 136:2

_____

_____

- 2 Corinthians 5:14

_____

_____

- 1 John 2:5

_____

_____

- 1 John 4:7

_____

_____

We could spend the rest of our lives trying to grasp God's banner of love over us and never exhaust it. What does Ephesians 3:17–19 say about the love of God through Christ for you and for me?

_____

_____

_____

What about when we fail, fall short, choose to sin? Do we, being evil in comparison, stop loving our own children when they fail us?

What is the truth of Romans 8:37–39?

_____

When we fail, He is just and faithful to restore us to right fellowship with Him through our confession and repentance (1 John 1:9). I pray today we would take the time to soak our souls in this rich and lavish love the Father holds out over our heads in the reality of the heavenlies that is far more real than the temporal images we see on earth. How can we not be compelled to share such a love with others?

DAY 4

Begin by prayerfully asking the Yahweh Nissi to reveal Himself to you through His Word. Then remember to practice saying your memory verse.

As we have learned, Yahweh Nissi is the banner of love over us to compel us to rally toward Him in Christ. We have victory in Him. The battle is His and He fights for us, but what does He expect of us?

Read 2 Samuel 22:31–36. He is our shield, and as we follow His ways we have victory; but what does verse 35 say about us?

God *trains us* for the battle. He expects us to show up! And fully armed and ready, I might add. My Bible's lexical aids say this about the word "train":

> It means to study, to learn, to teach, to instruct, to practice. It conveys the idea of both learning and educating. The starting point of knowledge is the fear (or reverential awe) of the Lord.[51]

It reminds me of the old proverb that says, "If the learner hasn't learned, the teacher hasn't taught." God *is* teaching. We are to make ourselves ready and study, learn and then practice His truths so we might be made ready for the battle around us (Ephesians 6:10–18).

It is a very real and literal battle that we, thankfully, are spared from seeing with mortal eyes. God is holding out a banner over believers in this battle that identifies us with "His side."

According to Ephesians 6:10–18, how do we "gear up"? List the various pieces of armor described and what they do.

_____

_____

_____

_____

_____

_____

Obviously, Paul's intention when writing this passage was not for us to physically wear armor. Although, sometimes I think getting that literal might help remind me of the spiritual truth here. But the intent is for us to gear up our minds with this truth and really know it.

- We are to surround our inner man with truth (Psalm 51:6).

- We are to guard our evil hearts with righteousness (Jeremiah 17:9).

- We are to use our feet to carry us to share the gospel and stand on its truth (Isaiah 52:7, Romans 10:15).

- We are to have faith when we cannot see (1 Corinthians 16:13, Hebrews 11:1).

- We are to live in the assurance of our salvation (1 John 5:12–13).

- We are to take up the sword of God's Word and know it, so we can fight well (Hebrews 4:12, Psalm 119:11).

- And we must pray, pray, pray (Ephesians 6:18).

Which of these do you need to work on practicing the most as you gear up for battle with the enemy?

_____

What will you do today to begin working on this?

_____

Begin by asking Yahweh Nissi to help you, as He who calls you will enable you! (1 Thessalonians 5:24)

DAY 5

Begin by prayerfully asking the Yahweh Nissi to reveal Himself to you through His Word. Then remember to practice saying your memory verse.

As we have met the Lord our Banner this week, we have seen both sides of this name. It is both a call to rally and a declaration of love and victory for God's people. Now we will see how unchangeable our God is that even the Son carries this symbol for us today.

Begin by reading Isaiah 11:10–12. What or who does this verse say will stand as a banner for the peoples?

_____

So who is this "Root of Jesse"? Read the parallel reference in Romans 15:12, and then read Revelation 5:5–6.

_____

Jesse was the father of King David who was of the line of Jesus (Luke 3:31). Jesus was the prophesied Root of Jesse that would stand as a banner for all people. Even before Jesus' feet walked on the sod of earth, God had a plan for all people to know Him, not just a call to the Jews. *New Illustrated Bible Commentary* says,

> The exalted Root of Jesse will attract the Gentiles to His resting place ... Banner is a rallying symbol. Jesus the Messiah is the banner for the gathering of peoples from all over the earth.[52]

So who is the banner over us? It is Jesus Himself. Why do you think this is so?

_____

_____

Jesus is the banner our Yahweh holds over His children. Jesus is our victory, our demonstration of God's love and our redemption.

Let's see this in Scripture. Keeping in mind what we have learned about the purpose for banners in battle; read each passage and write how Jesus is our banner in each example.

- 1 Corinthians 15:54–57

_____

- 1 John 5:4

_____

- Titus 2:13–14

_____

- Revelation 19:6–8

_____

Do you see Him? He is the banner over you even now, in the midst of your life, in the mundane tasks and necessary responsibilities of your day; Jesus is the banner over your head! How is your soul affected?

_____

_____

_____

If you are still struggling to grasp His love over you, His extension of victory and redemption, ask Him for eyes to see it. He desires us to drink in this truth into our inner man until we begin to live it out through submitting to our husband joyfully. We do it because we know the intense and completing love of Christ over us. We live it out through ministering cheerfully to our children and discipling them for Jesus. We live it out by having victory over the worries and anxieties that drag us down. We then begin to serve our neighbors, coworkers, and church family out of the overflow of redemption and compassion we know our Yahweh Nissi waves over us. Then we are truly living out an intimate knowledge of Yahweh Nissi, the LORD our Banner.

Take a moment to respond to what He has taught you through His word this week.

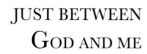

JUST BETWEEN
GOD AND ME

_____

_____

_____

_____

_____

_____

_____

_____

_____

_____

_____

_____

_____

_____

_____

_____

_____

_____

_____

_____

WHO IS EL ELYON?

As we come to the last week of study of these names of God, we approach the loftiest name of God. This week we will close with a name that clearly depicts His highness and majesty. I can't think of a more appropriate way to close our study of the names of God.

We have previously learned the Hebrew word for "god" is *El*. This can refer to the One True God or to manmade idols. The Hebrew word *elyon* comes from the root word meaning to ascend, to go up, rise, bring up, fill up, and to be high up or exalted. The word *elyon* refers to God as the Supreme Being and the Most High. The word signifies God's omnipotence, universality, and constancy. This name appears in Scripture two-thirds of the time as a proper name for God, denoting His exaltedness, supremacy, and overwhelming majesty. The name is usually translated in the English Bible as God Most High.

This name of God is first mentioned in Scripture in conjunction with the introduction of Melchizedek in Genesis 14:18. Melchizedek is a king and a high priest. He is thought by many scholars to be a pre-incarnate Christ, or in the very least an illustration of prophesy for the Christ. At any rate, this king blesses Abram in the name of the Most High, El Elyon, after Abram defeats a mighty army who has carried off Lot and his possessions (Genesis 14:8–20). In response to the king's blessing in verses 19–20, Abram gives a tenth of everything. This is a demonstration of Abram's faith and trust in the Lord Most High. He recognized that God alone was over all things. It was by His might that Abram could defeat the army and recover his nephew, Lot.

Abram goes on in faith to take an oath to El Elyon, the Creator of heaven and earth, to not accept anything from the king. Abram fully trusted God Most High to be fully in control over all things. God responds to Abram's faith in a big way as Genesis 15 opens with Yahweh speaking to Abram in a vision saying:

> I am your shield, your very great reward.

What a beautiful promise and confirmation that our God is Most High, and as we trust Him, He will guard us and be our provision.

Joseph in Genesis 45:5, 7–8 also knew this to be true of the Lord. Though he had been sold into slavery and thrown unfairly into jail, he trusted the one who is fully in control over all parts of Joseph's life. He could boldly look back over the course of his life with all the pain and all the unfair treatment and proclaim to his wicked brothers,

> You intended to harm me, but God intended it for good.
>
> Genesis 50:20

Whether or not he understood, Joseph knew God had a purpose in it all.

Can we boldly proclaim with Abram and Joseph that despite all the pain, unfairness, and mistreatment we have experienced, our God is the Most High? Have you ever considered that all the pain could be used to draw you nearer to the Lord and as a testimony to others? Let it not be in vain, but rather turning it over to the one who stands in control over all things with a perfect plan.

Read Psalm 57:2 and notice the reality of what God Most High does in the life of one who is willing.

> I cry out to God Most High, to God, who fulfills
> his purpose for me.

He does have a purpose and plan for your life that He thought of in advance. Cry out to Him to fulfill that purpose and give you eyes to see it come to fruition. His ways are good, and His plan is perfect. We can count on that.

DAY 1

MEMORY VERSE:

> For you, O LORD, are the Most High over all the
> earth; You are exalted far above all gods.
>
> Psalm 97:9

Begin today by asking the Lord Most High to reveal
the truths of His Word to you. Pray for a teachable
heart. Remember to practice your memory verse and
write it down on your index card to carry with you
this week.

As we begin to know God through His name El
Elyon, let's remind ourselves of the meaning of the
words. The prefix *El* expresses the same idea as in El
Shaddai; it means both God and might or power. The
word *Elyon* means "most high," every time it is used in
Scripture it is special and distinctive. It speaks of the
highest of a series or order of like natures; as in the
highest basket in a tier of baskets or nation above all
nations. It carries the meaning of sovereignty or over
all control.

Let's search out some of the verses that contain
"El Elyon" and see what we can uncover there.

According to Numbers 24:16, what do we receive from
the Most High?

Now read 2 Samuel 22:14–16 and note how the voice of the Most High has effect. What does it affect?

_____

_____

Look back at something interesting in this chapter. Read the words of David's song to the Lord here from verses 2–20. Why is the voice of the Most High resounding and causing the valleys to be exposed and the foundations of the earth to be laid bare? (See verse 4.)

_____

_____

Once the mighty, powerful El Elyon removes all obstacles and "reaches down" (verse 17), what does He do? And why, according to verse 20?

_____

_____

_____

Do you realize He feels the same way about you? He delights in those who are in awe of Him (Psalm 147:11). How does this affect your soul?

_____

_____

_____

Now let's try to catch another glimpse of the heart of the Most High. Read Lamentations 3:38 and fill in below:

> Is it not from the mouth of the _____ _____ that both _____ and _____ _____ come?

Can we accept this with trust? We know life is difficult. So if our God is the most high over all of it, couldn't He just make life easy and simple for us? For that matter, couldn't He just carry us home to glory when we place our faith in Him? He could, but would that bring Him glory and grow us to look increasingly like Jesus to a lost and dying world? John 3:16 says He desires none to perish, but all to come to everlasting life. How can that be if all believers were to just be raptured at the moment of salvation? He has a plan; our part is to trust Him.

We will look more into our role later, but for now thank Him for being trustworthy. He is the one who can increase your faith (Mark 9:24).

DAY 2

Begin today by asking the Lord Most High to reveal the truths of His Word to you. Pray for a teachable heart. Remember to practice your memory verse.

Today we will dig further into the meaning of El Elyon and try to catch a fresh perspective of the greatness of our God as we see all that is under His feet. As Andrew Jukes states in his book, *Names of God:*

> For the Most High doeth according to His will, in the armies of heaven, and among the inhabitants of the earth; and none can stay His hand or say unto Him, What doest Thou? His dominion is an everlasting dominion, and His kingdom is from generation to generation.[53]

So what could possibly be like Him and below Him? Remember we mentioned in yesterday's study that He is most high in relation to the nature of that which is beneath Him, as in the top basket in a stack of baskets. Keep that in mind as you ponder what He could be most high *of.* Begin by reading Isaiah 43:10.

Who is like Him?

_____

When Scripture reminds us of God's uniqueness, it is referring to His "Godness" or holiness, no one is like Him.

Yet, what does Genesis 1:26 say?

_____

So who carries the nature or image of God?

_____

So in the basket illustration, we are baskets and He is the top basket. He is the one over all, in every way. He does give us the free will to choose, but He is the sovereign one. We are created in His image and His likeness, but He is unique in His "Godness." Only He is God.

What else is He over? Read the following verses and note what they say He is over or superior to.

• Psalm 47:8

_____

• Psalm 89:11

_____

• Psalm 97:9

_____

If we know El Elyon is in sovereign control over all of this, what keeps us from believing He is in sovereign control over our lives?

_____

_____

_____

_____

If we do know He is in sovereign control in our life, then we must know that every detail of your life and of my life is sifted through His divine and perfect love for you and me. Read the following passages and make note of how God feels about you, His child.

- Psalm 22:8

_____

- Ephesians 1:7–8

_____

- Titus 3:7

_____

How do these truths affect your soul? Do you believe these are true of how God feels about you, personally? If not, how would you live differently if you did?

_____

_____

_____

DAY 3

Begin today by asking the Lord Most High to reveal the truths of His Word to you. Pray for a teachable heart. Remember to practice your memory verse.

Let's press further into El Elyon as we meet Him again in His interaction with Abram in Genesis 14. Begin by reading the chapter.

Through this chapter, God reveals Himself as El Elyon to Abram following his victory over the enemy kings of Persia and Chaldea.

According to verse 12, who did the enemy capture and carry off? And why was it significant to Abram?

_____

What was Abram's response?

_____

_____

After this incredible and very significant victory, an equally incredible and significant event happens to Abram. Who does he encounter? (v. 18 and v. 21)

_____

_____

Many mysterious truths have been studied about Melchizedek. What gifts does he come bearing to bless Abram?

_____

Why do you think these are significant?

_____

_____

Now read Luke 22:17–20, and record what might be the significance of the bread and wine as pertaining to this passage.

_____

_____

_____

Many believe Melchizadek to have been a pre-incarnate Christ. There is no recorded history for him, which was incredibly unique, since kings had to be *proven* royal blood. God is making a point here with this priest king blessing Abram with bread and wine. What blessing does he pronounce over Abram? Who does he claim the blessing from?

_____

_____

In turn, when speaking to the second king who tries to bribe him, Abram claims the same name of God over the situation (Genesis 14:22–23). Abram's act of taking nothing from this second king demonstrates his faith in his El Elyon. He knew El Elyon as his God, sovereign and supreme over every detail of his life. For him, there was no choice between earthly reliance and God reliance; Abram chose to rely on God.

Do you remember what Romans 15:4 says of these Old Testament stories?

Because of this, many Old Testament battles are examples of our own battles with the enemies of the world, our flesh, and Satan. Which of these are you currently battling?

If you feel you are not in a battle right now, it is your season to prepare because a battle is coming. Such is life. But praise God, He is our El Elyon and in sovereign control over those battles and victories, when we press into His side and trust Him for the victory.

Take your current battles to the Lord in prayer, remembering He is a warrior who fights for you (Exodus 15:3).

DAY 4

Begin today by asking the Lord Most High to reveal the truths of His Word to you. Pray for a teachable heart. Remember to practice your memory verse.

The psalmist paints a beautiful picture of the Most High through Psalm 91. We studied this psalm a few weeks ago, but I pray it falls afresh over you as you witness the sovereign finger of El Elyon through it.

Read Psalm 91.

This psalm opens with two names we are now familiar with. What are they?

_____

One commentary says of these names used in conjunction with one another here speaks of God's mountain-like majesty.[54] He is the one over all. This is a beautiful psalm often used in prayer for protection for others. It is important to remember that God does allow pain into our lives for His many purposes, one of which is to make us holy.

What does this psalm say God does or will do?

_____

_____

_____

_____

_____

Who will He do that for? (See verses 1, 2, 9, and 14.)

_____

_____

_____

_____

It is important to realize that often what we wish was physical has a much richer spiritual connotation. Paul (from the New Testament) loved the Lord, the disciples loved the Lord, the men and women listed in "the Hall of Faith" (of Hebrews 11) loved the Lord, yet what does Hebrews 11:39 say of the Old Testament saints?

_____

_____

So how were they protected? Believers who follow Jesus fervently are currently being persecuted and killed all over this world. Children of God are diagnosed with cancer, stolen from, lied to, betrayed, and in immense pain. Read Hebrews 11:32–40 slowly now. Let the truth here sink into your heart.

These saints of old knew something we often forget. This life is temporal! It might feel good sometimes, be comfortable and even joyful, but God allows the pain, heartache, and death to remind us of the "something better" (v. 40) He has planned.

How do we connect the pain we feel with the truths of Psalm 91?

_____

_____

God protects us spiritually. Such a war is going on right now over our heads, we cannot even fathom. He is guarding you under His wing. He holds your salvation secure. He is your fortress to run to when this life gets unbearable. We can live without the fear of death because there is a greater truth at work.

Glance back to Psalm 91. What does the psalmist (or we) have to do in order to rest in His shadow and be protected by His wings? (v. 1, 9)

_____

The word translated "dwell" in verse 1 is the Hebrew word *yasab,* meaning to dwell whether literally or figuratively. It can indicate a lengthy residence. How about an eternal one? Praise God when we come into relationship with Him through His Son, we are secure in that for eternity.

What does the Lord say in verse 14? Fill in the verse.

> "Because he _____ Me," says the Lord, "I will rescue him, I will protect him."

The word here for love is not the usual word used for love in the Old Testament. Instead it carries the idea of "holding close to" even "hugging tightly in love." Isn't that a great visual? When we hug tightly in love to our Savior, He rescues us. It reminds me of a young child in the pool for the first time. They cling tightly don't they? In return, we hold them and protect them from drowning or even splashes that may prevent them from ever returning to the pool cheerfully. We have the "power" to drop the child in the pool or rescue the child. El Elyon is the one with the power and sovereign control. He chooses to rescue those who love Him and cling to Him.

In verse 15, what does El Elyon go on to promise about those who call on Him?

_____

_____

_____

Your El Elyon loves you fervently and with passion. He desires your whole heart and mind. He desires to protect you and guard you. You need only call out and cling to Him. Praise Him regarding what He has spoken through Psalm 91 to you.

Begin today by asking the Lord Most High to reveal the truths of His Word to you. Pray for a teachable heart. Remember to practice your memory verse.

So, how does Jesus, the Word made flesh to dwell among us, fulfill El Elyon's character? In John 14:9 Jesus declared that if we see Him, we see the Father. Many of the names the Father reveals Himself as Jesus also revealed as part of His own character. El Elyon is one of those names.

Begin by reading Colossians 1:15–20. Who does it say is the very image of the invisible God?

The word for "image" here is referring to a facsimile of God. It is speaking of an actual prototype. Jesus *is* God in human likeness. My firstborn son looks a lot like me. He is made in my "image", but he is not actually me. We are images of our Creator and bear marks of His creation, but we are not God. Jesus, on the other hand, does not bear marks of "Godness"; He *is* God.

In Colossians 1:15, the English reference to "first-born" is not referring to Jesus being the first thing God made. Jesus was never *made;* He is the eternal God (see John 1). The Greek word *prototokos* for "first-born" here means first in *place,* as in preeminence. The idea of firstborn in the Hebrew culture often meant the firstborn son was the rightful heir to the line of his father. Although being firstborn referred more to rank and privilege than to order of birth. Since Christ is God, He is supreme in rank over all creation. Yet He is not only the transcendent deity who created us; He is the one who died on our behalf (Philippians 2:6–18) and was subsequently raised from the dead. Thus, He is also the firstborn from the dead (v. 18), the first one who experienced the true resurrection (1 Corinthians 15:20).

Read Matthew 28:18. What has Jesus been given?

_____

Jesus is the rightful heir of His Father's kingdom. He has supremacy and authority over all things, as given by God the Father. Jesus is our New Testament El Elyon.

According to Colossians 1:18–20 God placed Jesus "first place" for a purpose. What is that purpose?

_____

_____

God is always after a relationship with His children. He desires intimacy with you above all else. Our relationship requires holiness on our part because He is holy and we are fallen sinners (Romans 3:23). Through the shed blood of Christ on the cross, we are reconciled to a holy God for the purpose of intimate relationship.

So the question remains, is Christ first place in our life? Does He consume our thoughts? Our hearts? Our activity? Are we living our lives unto Him alone?

Jesus *is* the Most High God, but is He "most high" in your life? Is He your heart's desire? Spend some time right now asking Him to reveal your deepest desires to you. Be willing to humble yourself before Him and confess those things which have taken preeminence in your life. Ask Him to become the Most High in your heart and life. Write out how you will *practically* work on giving Jesus first place in your thoughts and life in the days and weeks to come (morning quiet times, memorizing Scripture, prayer, etc.).

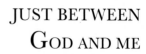

JUST BETWEEN
GOD AND ME

A FINAL WORD

As we close this journey through some of the names of God, I pray we come to this place changed and a bit more confident in who our God is. We have seen Hebrews 13:8 come to life for us. "Jesus Christ is the same yesterday and today and forever." God's deity has been displayed for us from Genesis to Revelation with perfect consistency.

Let's take with us the truths we have sown into our hearts and know that eternal life, as described in John 17:3, is knowing the only true God. I pray you know Him better now than you did ten weeks ago, when you embarked on this journey. More importantly, I pray you are confidently living out that wisdom in your daily life. As we conclude this study, we can know that our adventure with the Lord Jesus has only begun. Knowing Him *is* life and life abundantly! Go forth in that confidence and blessing, dear reader, our Lord has much to reveal. Thank you for walking this portion of the path with me.

ENDNOTES

1   Nancy Leigh DeMoss. *Lies Women Believe.* (Chicago, IL: Moody Bible Institute, 2001) 31.

2   Nathan Stone. *Names of God.* (Chicago, IL: The Moody Bible Institute, 1944) 9.

3   Spiros Zodhiates, Th.D. Old Testament Lexical Aids. *Key Word Study Bible.* (Chattanooga, TN: AMG Publishers, 1996) 1520.

4   Ibid, 1511.

5   Ibid, 1504.

6   Ibid, 1542.

7   Ibid, 1508.

8   Ibid, 1521.

9   Ibid, 1504, 1507, 1520.

10 Andrew Jukes. *Names of God.* (Grand Rapids, MI: Kregel Publications, 1967) 25.

11 Stone, 13.

12 Jukes, 19.

13 Jennifer Kennedy Dean. *The Life-Changing Power in the Name of Jesus.* (Birmingham, AL: New Hope Publishers, 2004) 80.

14 Ibid.

15 Ibid, 74.

16 AW Tozer. *The Pursuit of God*. (Camp Hill, PA: Christian Publications, 1993)

17 HebrewforChristians.com

18 Stone, 19.

19 Catherine Martin. *Trusting in the Names of God*. (Eugene, OR: Harvest House Publishers, 2008) 123.

20 Ibid, 124.

21 Stone, 43.

22 Ann Spangler. *Praying the Names of God*. (Grand Rapids, MI: Zondervan, 2004) 92.

23 Kay Arthur. *Lord, I Want to Know You*. (Colorado Springs, CO: Waterbrook Press, 2001) 39.

24 Lexical Aids, 1544.

25 Dean, 49.

26 Jukes, 66.

27 Warren Baker and Eugene Carpenter, ed. *The Complete Word Study Dictionary of the Old Testament*. (Chattanooga, TN: AMG Publishers, 2003) 952.

28 John F Walvoord and Roy B Zuck, ed. *The Bible Knowledge Commentary*. (Wheaton, IL: Victor Books, 1985) 1044.

29 Lexical Aids, 1630.

30 Ibid.

31 Dean, 51.

32 Lexical Aids, 1544.

33 Stone, 140.

34 Harriet-Louise H Patterson. *Around the Mediterranean with My Bible*. Patterson PR.

35 Lexical Aids, 1556.

36 Brother Lawrence. *The Practice of the Presence of God*. (Grand Rapids, MI: Spire Books, 1967) 89–90.

37 Ann Spangler. *Praying the Names of God*. (Grand Rapids, MI: Zondervan Publishers, 2004) 106.

38 Beth Moore. *Living Beyond Yourself.* (Nashville, TN: Lifeway Publishers, 1998) 98.

39 Ibid, 99.

40 Stone, 149.

41 Ibid, 23.

42 Spiros Zodhiates, gen. ed. *The Complete Word Study Dictionary of the New Testament*. (Chattanooga, TN: AMG Publishers, 1993) 1295.

43 Lexical Aids, 1650.

44 Ibid, 1979, 1980.

45 Ibid, 1522.

46 Ibid, 1527.

47 Ibid, 1556.

48 Scriven, Joseph. "What a Friend We Have in Jesus." 1855.

49 Lexical Aids, 1501.

50 Ibid, 1525.

51 Radmacher, Earl, gen. ed. *New Illustrated Bible Commentary*. (Nashville, TN: Nelson Publishers, 1999), 821.

52 Jukes, 88–89.

53 Radmacher, 709.